Tramp for the Lord

Further copies of this book can be obtained from
Christian Literature Crusade Bookshops

Other titles by Corrie ten Boom

The Hiding Place
Amazing Love
Common Sense Not Needed
Defeated Enemies
Marching Orders for the End Battle
Not Good If Detached
A Prisoner and Yet ...
Plenty for Everyone

Christian Literature Crusade,
The Dean, Alresford, Hants.
Please write for catalogue and further details

CORRIE TEN BOOM

WITH JAMIE BUCKINGHAM

Tramp for the Lord

HODDER AND STOUGHTON
LONDON SYDNEY AUCKLAND TORONTO
and
CHRISTIAN LITERATURE CRUSADE
LONDON

Unless otherwise identified, Scripture references in this book are from the King James Version of the Bible.

Scripture references identified PHILLIPS are from The New Testament in Modern English translated by J. B. Phillips, 1958.

Scripture references identified NEB are from *The New English Bible*. Copyright © The Delegates of the Oxford University Press and the Syndics of the Cambridge University Press 1961 and 1970. Reprinted by permission.

Scripture references identified LB are from The Living Bible. Copyright © 1971 by Tyndale House Publishers, Wheaton, Illinois 60187. All rights reserved.

The poem 'Royal Scars' is from *Wings* by Amy Carmichael published by SPCK, London.

Excerpt from *War on the Saints* by Jessie Penn-Lewis. The Overcomer Literature Trust, Parkstone, Poole, and Christian Literature Crusade, Fort Washington. Used by permission.

Contents

Foreword

My wife Jackie and I met Tante (Aunt) Corrie and her pretty, blond secretary, Ellen de Kroon, at the airport in Melbourne, Florida. Ellen had called the night before saying they were flying in, but that Corrie had been having some severe heart pains. At eighty years of age, that's serious business.

We met the plane and whisked them to our house which is just minutes from the airport 'I'm very tired,' Tante Corrie said. 'I like to rest a while.'

Moments later she was stretched out on our daughter's lavender bedspread. I opened the window so the soft, tropical breeze could blow in from the lake behind the house. Gently closing the door, I cautioned the children to speak in whispers, and tiptoed into the kitchen to join Jackie and Ellen.

Ellen had brought us some Gouda cheese and we sliced it, reminiscing over my first meal in Corrie's house in Holland. Ellen couldn't wait to tell Jackie about the expression on my face when Corrie informed me I had a choice of two dishes for lunch: raw mullet dipped in onion, or smoked eel.

Talking softly and munching on cheese and crackers, I glanced up to see Tante Corrie coming down the hall, her eyes sparkling.

'Aren't you going to rest?' I asked.

'Oh, I have already a good sleep,' she answered in her thick, Dutch accent. 'Ten minutes is all you need when God gives the sleep.'

It is this remarkable power of recuperation which has allowed Tante Corrie, at more than eighty years of age, to tramp the world for the Lord. I saw that same power at work in her life a year later in Pittsburgh. We were both on the programme for a Bible conference at the Pittsburgh Theological Seminary. She had spoken three times that day to a congregation made up of everybody from bearded Jesus People to university professors. I was out late that night and, when I returned to the dormitory, I saw Ellen running down the hall 'Tante Corrie is having a heart attack,' she said

I raced to Corrie's room. She was stretched out on her bed, her face grey from the pain 'God has told me my time is not yet up,' she whispered. 'I have sent for a minister to pray that I may be healed.'

Moments later, as the young minister arrived and laid his hands on her, I saw her features relax and the colour return to her cheeks. 'Thank You, Lord,' she said softly, 'for taking away the pain.' Then, signifying she was ready for us to leave, she said, 'I go to sleep now.'

The next morning at eight o'clock she was behind the pulpit speaking to a thousand persons in the great auditorium — as though nothing extraordinary had happened.

I am convinced that the secret of Tante Corrie's great recuperative power, as well as the secret of her popularity as a speaker, lies in her childlikeness. As a little girl believes her Daddy can do anything, so Corrie ten Boom trusts in God — even more. She is living proof of what happens when a woman — when *any* person — is filled with the Holy Spirit.

JAMIE BUCKINGHAM

*I will teach you, and guide you in the way you
should go. I will keep you under my eye.*

Psalms 32:8 NEB

Introduction: The World Is My Classroom

The school of life offers some difficult courses, but it is in the
difficult class that one learns the most — especially when
your teacher is the Lord Jesus Himself.

The hardest lessons for me were in a cell with four walls.
The cell in the prison at Scheveningen, Holland, was six
paces in length, two paces in breadth, with a door that could
be opened only from the outside. Later there were four
barbed-wire fences, charged with electricity, enclosing a
concentration camp in Germany. The gates were manned by
guards with loaded machine guns. It was there in Ravensbruck that more than ninety-six thousand women
died.

After that time in prison, the entire world became my
classroom. Since World War II, I have travelled around it
twice, speaking in more than sixty countries on all con-
tinents. During these three decades I have become familiar
with airports, bus stations, and passport offices. Under me
have been wheels of every description: wheels of auto-
mobiles, trains, jinrikishas, horse-drawn wagons, and the
landing gear of airplanes. Wheels, wheels, wheels! Even the
wheels of wheelchairs.

I have enjoyed hospitality in a great number of homes and have slept in many times more than a thousand beds. Sometimes I have slept in comfortable beds with foam rubber mattresses in the United States, and sometimes on straw mats on dirt floors in India. There have been clean rooms and dirty rooms.

One bathroom in Hollywood had a view of exotic plants and flowers from the sunken Roman bathtub; while a bathroom in Borneo was simply a mud hut equipped with nothing but a barrel of cold water. Once, while staying with a group of young Jewish girls in Israel, I had to climb over a mountain of building materials, and walk through a junk-filled field to make my way to a tiny outhouse which was nothing more than a hole in the ground. Such a place would have been impossible to find at night.

Always in my travels, even now that I am in my ninth decade of life, I have carried in my hand and in my heart the Bible — the very Word of Life which is almost bursting with Good News. And there has been plenty for everyone. I often feel as the disciples must have felt as they fed more than five thousand with five loaves and two fishes. The secret was that they had received it from the blessed hand of the Master. There was abundance for all and twelve basketfuls of fragments left over.

There has been plenty for the dying ones in the concentration camps — plenty for the thousands gathered in universities, in town halls, and in churches all over the world. Sometimes I have spoken to a few men in prison who stood behind bars and listened hungrily. Once to a group of six missionaries in Japan who offered me hospitality during a twenty-eight-hour rainstorm in which more than a thousand persons perished around us. Groups of hundreds and crowds of thousands have listened under pandals in India and in theatres in South America. I have spoken to tens of

10

thousands at one time in the giant stadiums of America and retreated to the mountains of North Carolina to spend time with a small group of girls in a summer camp.

'God so loved the world . . .' (John 3:16) Jesus said. And that is why I keep going, even into my eightieth years, because we've a story to tell to the nations, a story of love and light.

God has plans — not problems — for our lives. Before she died in the concentration camp in Ravensbruck, my sister Betsie said to me, 'Corrie, your whole life has been a training for the work you are doing here in prison — and for the work you will do afterward.'

The life of a Christian is an education for higher service. No athlete complains when the training is hard. He thinks of the game, or the race. As the Apostle Paul wrote:

In my opinion, whatever we may have to go through now is less than nothing compared with the magnificent future God has planned for us. The whole creation is on tiptoe to see the wonderful sight of the sons of God coming into their own. The world of creation cannot as yet see reality, not because it chooses to be blind, but because in God's purpose it has been so limited — yet it has been given hope. And the hope is that in the end the whole of created life will be rescued from the tyranny of change and decay and have its share in that magnificent liberty which can only belong to the children of God!

It is plain to anyone with eyes to see that at the present time all created life groans in a sort of universal travail. And it is plain, too, that we who have a foretaste of the Spirit are in a state of painful tension, while we wait for that redemption of our bodies which will mean that at last we have realized our full sonship in him.

Romans 8:18–23 PHILLIPS

Looking back across the years of my life, I can see the working of a divine pattern which is the way of God with His children. When I was in a prison camp in Holland during the war, I often prayed, 'Lord, never let the enemy put me in a German concentration camp.' God answered *no* to that prayer. Yet in the German camp, with all its horror, I found many prisoners who had never heard of Jesus Christ. If God had not used my sister Betsie and me to bring them to Him, they would never have heard of Him. Many died, or were killed, but many died with the Name of Jesus on their lips. They were well worth all our suffering. Faith is like radar which sees through the fog — the reality of things at a distance that the human eye cannot see.

My life is but a weaving, between my God and me,
I do not choose the colours, He worketh steadily,
Oftimes He weaveth sorrow, and I in foolish pride,
Forget He sees the upper, and I the underside.
Not till the loom is silent, and shuttles cease to fly,
Will God unroll the canvas and explain the reason why
The dark threads are as needful in the skilful Weaver's
    hand,
As the threads of gold and silver in the pattern He has
    planned.

ANONYMOUS

Although the threads of my life have often seemed knotted, I know, by faith, that on the other side of the embroidery there is a crown. As I have walked the world — a tramp for the Lord — I have learned a few lessons in God's great classroom. Even as I share these things with those of you who read this book, I pray the Holy Spirit will reveal something of the divine pattern in God's plan for you also.

CORRIE TEN BOOM
Baarn, Holland

*My brethren, count it all joy when you fall into
[difficult times]. Knowing this, that the trying
of your faith worketh patience.*

James 1:2, 3

1   A Strange Place to Hope

Rank upon rank we stood that hot September morning in
1944, more than a thousand women lining the railroad
siding, one unspoken thought among us: *Not Germany!*

Beside me my sister Betsie swayed. I was fifty-two, Betsie
fifty-nine. These seven months in a prison and concentration
camp since we had been caught concealing Jews in our home
had been harder on her. But prisoners though we were, at
least till now we had remained in Holland. And now when
liberation must come any day, where were they taking us?

Behind us guards were shouting, prodding us with their
guns. Instinctively my hand went to the string around my
neck. From it, hanging down my back between my shoulder
blades, was the small cloth bag that held our Bible, that
forbidden Book which had not only sustained Betsie and me
throughout these months, but given us strength to share with
our fellow prisoners. So far we had kept it hidden. But if we
should go to Germany ... We had heard tales of the prison
inspections there.

A long line of empty boxcars was rolling slowly past.
Now they clanged to a halt and a gaping freight door
loomed in front of us. I helped Betsie over the steep side.

13

The dark boxcar grew quickly crowded. We were pressed against the wall. It was a small European freight car; thirty or forty people jammed it. And still the guards drove women in, pushing, jabbing with their guns. It was only when eighty women were packed inside that the heavy door slid shut and we heard the iron bolts driven into place outside.

Women were sobbing and many fainted, although in the tightly wedged crowd they remained upright. The sun beat down on the motionless train; the temperature in the packed car rose. It was hours before the train gave a sudden lurch and began to move. Almost at once it stopped again, then again crawled forward. The rest of that day and all night long it was the same — stopping, starting, slamming, jerking. Once through a slit in the side of the car I saw trainmen carrying a length of twisted rail. Maybe the tracks ahead were destroyed. Maybe we would still be in Holland when the liberation came.

But at dawn we rolled through the Dutch border town of Emmerich. We were in Germany.

For two more incredible days and two more nights we were carried deeper and deeper into the land of our fears. Worse than the crush of bodies and the filth, was the thirst. Two or three times when the train was stopped the door was slid open a few inches and a pail of water passed in. But we had become animals, incapable of plan. Those near the door got it all.

At last, on the morning of the third day, the door was hauled open its full width. Only a handful of very young soldiers was there to order us out and march us off. No more were needed. We could scarcely walk, let alone resist. From the crest of a small hill we saw it — the end of our journey — a vast gray barracks city surrounded by double concrete walls.

'Ravensbruck!'

Like a whispered curse, the word passed back through the line. This was the notorious women's death camp itself, the very symbol to Dutch hearts of all that was evil. As we stumbled down the hill, I felt the little Bible bumping on my back. As long as we had that, I thought, we could face even hell itself. But how could we conceal it through the inspection I knew lay ahead?

It was the middle of the night when Betsie and I reached the processing barracks. And there, under the harsh ceiling lights, we saw a dismaying sight. As each woman reached the head of the line she had to strip off ever scrap of clothes, throw them all onto a pile guarded by soldiers, and walk naked past the scrutiny of a dozen guards into the shower room. Coming out of the shower room she wore only a thin regulation prison dress and a pair of shoes.

Our Bible! How could we take it past so many watchful eyes?

'Oh, Betsie!' I began — and then stopped at the sight of her pain-whitened face. As a guard strode by, I begged him in German to show us the toilets. He jerked his head in the direction of the shower room. 'Use the drain holes!' he snapped.

Timidly Betsie and I stepped out of line and walked forward to the huge room with its row on row of overhead spigots. It was empty, waiting for the next batch of fifty naked and shivering women.

A few minutes later we would return here stripped of everything we possessed. And then we saw them, stacked in a corner, a pile of old wooden benches crawling with cockroaches, but to us the furniture of heaven itself.

In an instant I had slipped the little bag over my head and, along with my woolen underwear, had stuffed it behind the benches.

And so it was that when we were herded into that room

ten minutes later, we were not poor, but rich — rich in the care of Him who was God even of Ravensbruck.

Of course when I put on the flimsy prison dress, the Bible bulged beneath it. But that was His business, not mine. At the exit, guards were feeling every prisoner, front, back, and sides. I prayed, 'Oh, Lord, send your angels to surround us.' But then I remembered that angels are spirits and you can see through them. What I needed was an angel to shield me so the guards could not see me. 'Lord,' I prayed again, 'make your angels untransparent.' How unorthodox you can pray when you are in great need! But God did not mind. He did it.

The woman ahead of me was searched. Behind me, Betsie was searched. They did not touch or even look at me. It was as though I was blocked out of their sight.

Outside the building was a second ordeal, another line of guards examining each prisoner again. I slowed down as I reached them, but the captain shoved me roughly by the shoulder. 'Move along! You're holding up the line.'

So Betsie and I came to our barracks at Ravensbruck. Before long we were holding clandestine Bible study groups for an ever-growing group of believers, and Barracks 28 became known throughout the camp as 'the crazy place, where they hope'.

Yes, hoped, in spite of all that human madness could do. We had learned that a stronger power had the final word, even here.

(Reprinted by permission from GUIDEPOSTS MAGAZINE, Copyright 1972 by Guideposts Associates, Inc., Carmel, New York 10512.)

*. . . and . . . you shall be My witnesses both
in Jerusalem, and in all Judea, and Samaria. . . .*

Acts 1:8 RSV

2   Witnesses Unto Me

It was a week after Betsie had died in Ravensbruck that I
took my place in the ranks of women prisoners standing
together in the icy cold of the early morning.

'66730!'

'That is my number,' I said weakly as we took our places
for roll call.

'ten Boom, Cornelia.'

'That is my name,' I thought. How strange that they
would call me by name when they always addressed us by
number!

'Come forward.'

We were falling in line for the roll call. Ten in a line, every
one hundredth woman one step forward. My friends looked
at me sadly.

'What does it mean?' I asked inwardly. 'Punishment . . .
freedom . . . the gas chamber . . . sent to another concentration camp?'

There was but one thought that comforted me. 'What a
joy that Betsie is in heaven. No matter what terrible things
now happen, she will not have to bear it.'

The guard, a young German girl, shouted at me. 'Nr.
66730!'

I stepped forward, stood at attention and repeated the necessary words. '*Schutzhaftling ten Boom, Cornelia, meldet sich.*'

'Stand on Number 1 on the roll call.'

I went to the place to the far right, where I could overlook the entire square of the bleak camp. Standing in the crowd I could not feel the draft, but now, standing in the bitter cold, the wind whipped through my ragged prison dress. Another girl, young and frightened, was sent to stand beside me. Roll call took three hours and we were almost frozen. She saw how cold I was and rubbed my spine when the guards were not looking.

'Why must I stand here?' I asked through chattering teeth.

Her answer was barely audible as it came from her blue lips. 'Death sentence.'

I turned back to the Lord. 'Perhaps I'll see you soon face-to-face, like Betsie does now, Lord. Let it not be too cruel a killing. Not gas, Lord, nor hanging. I prefer shooting. It is so quick. You see something, you hear something, and it is finished.'

I looked back at the young girl beside me. 'Lord, this is perhaps the last chance I will have to bring someone to You before I arrive in heaven. Use me, Lord. Give me all the love and wisdom I need.'

'What is your name?' I asked her softly, glancing always to see if the guards were looking.

'Tiny.'

'I am Corrie,' I whispered. 'How long have you been here?'

'Two years.'

'Did you ever read the Bible?'

'No, I never did.'

'Do you believe God exists?'

18

'I do. I wish I knew more about Him. Do you know Him?'

'I do. Jesus, His Son, came to this world to carry our punishment. He died on the cross, but He rose from the dead and has promised to be with us always. My sister died here. She suffered so much. I, too, have suffered. But Jesus is always with us. He did a miracle in taking away all my hatred and bitterness for my enemies. Jesus is willing to bring into our hearts God's love through His Holy Spirit.'

Tiny listened. For almost three hours we talked while the guards completed the roll call. It was a miracle, for I had a chance to explain many things about Jesus. The prisoners behind us listened, too. I felt happy. Perhaps this was my last chance in life, but what joy!

I continued. 'Jesus wants to live in your heart. "Behold, I stand at the door and knock", He says. "If anyone opens the door, I'll come in." Will you open the door of your heart and let Him come in and change you?'

'I will,' she said.

'Then talk to Him. Tell Him whatever you think. Now you have a Friend who never leaves you alone.'

The siren sounded and the guards shouted at the prisoners. 'Get to work!'

Thousands of women prisoners were running to their places where they had to march to their work. Tiny disappeared from sight. Only I was left standing in my place where I had been ordered not to move. I still did not know what fate awaited me.

I did know, however, that the God who never slumbers nor sleeps was now with Tiny. And Tiny knew it, too. Neither of us knew at that time how important that was going to be to her in the next few days. But above the din of the concentration camp, I thought I heard the singing of the angels.

19

Then I heard my name called. Was it death? Oh, thank God, no. It was life. I was being released. I later learned it was through an administrative blunder, but even then I knew it was not the end of an era — it was just the beginning. Ahead of me was the world.

*Then he turned my sorrow into joy! He took
away my clothes of mourning . . . .*

Psalms 30:11 LB

3 Release!

When you are dying — when you stand at the gate of eternity — you see things from a different perspective than when you think you may live for a long time. I had been standing at that gate for many months, living in Barracks 28 in the shadow of the crematorium. Every time I saw the smoke pouring from the hideous smokestacks I knew it was the last remains of some poor women who had been with me in Ravensbruck. Often I asked myself, 'When will it be my time to be killed or die?'

But I was not afraid. Following Betsie's death, God's Presence was even more real. Even though I was looking into the valley of the shadow of death, I was not afraid. It is here that Jesus comes the closest, taking our hand, and leading us through.

One week before the order came to kill all the women of my age, I was free. I still do not understand all the details of my release from Ravensbruck. All I know is, it was a miracle of God.

I stood in the prison yard — waiting the final order. Beyond the walls with their strands of barbed wire stood the silent trees of the German forest, looking so much like the grey-green sets on the back of one of our theatre stages in Holland.

Mimi, one of the fellow prisoners, came within whispering distance. 'Tiny died this morning,' she said without looking at me. 'And Marie also.'

Tiny! 'Oh, Lord, thank You for letting me point her to Jesus who has now ushered her safely into Your Presence.' And Marie. I knew her well. She lived in my barracks and had attended my Bible talks. Like Tiny, Marie had also accepted Jesus as her Lord. I looked back at the long rows of barracks. 'Lord, if it was only for Tiny and Marie — that they might come to know You before they died — then it was all worthwhile.'

A guard spoke harshly, telling Mimi to leave the yard. Then he said to me, 'Face the gate. Do not turn around.'

The gate swung open and I glimpsed the lake in front of the camp. I could smell freedom.

'Follow me,' a young girl in an officer's uniform said to me.

I walked slowly through the gate, never looking back. Behind me I heard the hinges squeak as the gate swung shut. I was free, and flooding through my mind were the words of Jesus to the church at Philadelphia:

Behold, I have set before thee an open door, and no man can shut it . . .

Revelation 3:8

First that door directed me back to Holland. The train ride took three days. Another prisoner, Claire Prins, had been released with me. Her leg was alarmingly swollen and of course both of us were mere skin and bones. But we were *free*!

Arriving in Groningen, we made our way to a Christian

hospital called the Deaconess House, where I asked to speak to the superintendent. Perhaps they would help us until I could return to Haarlem, I thought.

'Sister Tavenier cannot come at the moment,' the attendant said. 'She is helping conduct a Christian service in one of the wards. I'm afraid you will have to wait.'

'Would you mind,' I said, looking at the attendant, 'if I attended the service also?'

She looked at me tenderly, sensing, perhaps, some of my suffering. 'Why, of course. You may rest in the waiting room until it starts. I'll come after you.'

'Nurse . . .,' I hesitated to ask, 'have you anything for me to drink?'

Again the look of compassion crossed her face. 'I'll bring you some tea,' she said gently.

A few minutes later she placed it before me, saying, 'I have not put butter on the toast for I see you are sick. The dry toast and tea will be good for you.'

I was deeply touched by this tiny show of consideration. A moment later I was lying in a comfortable chair with my legs outstretched on a bench. A wonderful feeling of rest descended on me. I was in the Netherlands, among good people. My suffering was over.

A nurse came for me, to take me to the ward where the service was to be held. Chairs had been arranged in a semi-circle between the beds, facing a table. An elderly minister walked in and a hymnal was handed me. I could see the nurses and patients glancing stealthily at me. My clothes were ragged and filthy, hanging from my gaunt body like rags on a scarecrow. Yet I was so thankful to be free I cared not.

The minister spoke in a well-modulated voice. Then we joined in singing. I could not help but make comparisons: the dirty prison dormitory, infection-ridden and filthy, the beds full of lice, and now this. Clean sheets and pillow cases and a spotless floor. The hoarse voices of the slave drivers and the mature, melodious voice of the minister. Only the singing was the same, for we had sung at Ravensbruck. Singing was one of the ways we kept up our courage.

Following the service the nurse took me to the superintendent's office. 'Miss Prins has been taken care of,' she said, 'and is already in a fresh bed. You both must have had a horrible experience. But now, what must be done with you?'

I sat in a chair across from her desk. For more than a year I had not been allowed to make a decision. All I could do was follow orders. It was difficult even to think. 'I don't know, Sister,' I said. It was enough just to be surrounded by people who were not angry with me.

'I know what,' she said, as she touched a bell. 'First we'll give you a warm dinner.'

A young nurse appeared and took my arm, guiding me down a hall towards the dining room. 'I understand you have just been released from Ravensbruck,' she said. 'Where are you going? Where is your home?'

'I am going to Haarlem,' I replied.

'Oh, Haarlem,' she said with excitement. 'Do you know Corrie ten Boom who lives there?'

I looked at her. She was one of the YWCA leaders I had worked with before the war. 'Truus Benes!' I exclaimed in delight.

'Why, yes, that is my name,' she said, bewildered. 'But I don't believe I know you.'

'I am Corrie ten Boom.'

The nurse stopped abruptly in the hall, staring at me. 'Oh, no, that is impossible. I know Corrie ten Boom very well. I have been in girls' camps with her several times. She is much younger than you.'

'But, really, I am Corrie ten Boom,' I argued. Then I thought of how I must have looked. My face was thin and pale, my mouth wide, like skin stretched across a skull. My hair fell queerly about my face. My eyes were hollow. My coat was dirty, for I had at times slept on the floor of the train as we travelled out of Germany. The belt of my dress sagged, for I had not had the energy to fasten it.

The nurse reached out tenderly and touched my chapped hand. 'Yes ... yes ... it is you. It *is*!' And then we both broke into laughter.

In the dining room we sat opposite each other at a small table and I asked about our mutual acquaintances. Was Mary Barger still living? Jeanne Blooker and ...? It was ridiculous to ask such questions, but I wanted to know everything. The world, for me, had stopped while I had been in the concentration camp. Now it was beginning to turn again and I had so much catching up to do.

Then I was eating. Potatoes, brussels sprouts, meat and gravy, and for dessert, pudding with currant juice and an apple!

'I have never seen anyone eat so intensely,' one of the nurses from a nearby table commented. I cared not. With every mouthful of food I could feel new life streaming into my body. I had once said to Betsie in camp, 'When we get home we shall have to eat carefully, taking only small amounts at a time until our stomachs are ready.'

'No,' Betsie had said, 'God will see to it that we shall be able to retain all sorts of food right from the start.'

She was right. How wonderfully good that food did taste. I shall remember that meal as long as I live.

Then came a warm bath. They could hardly get me out of it. My poor sick skin, damaged by lice, seemed to grow softer the moment I slipped into that warm tub.

Afterwards they dressed me. Several of the ex-leaders of

the Netherlands Girls' Clubs were among the nurses — girls that I had known before the war. They dressed me up as if I were a doll. One of them had lingerie, another shoes, another a dress and pins for my hair. I felt so happy that I laughed for sheer joy. How sweet they were to me.

These young women had been trained in kindness. How opposite from the concentration camp where men had been trained in cruelty.

I was then taken to a cozy bedroom so I could rest. How lovely was the combination of colours. I was starved for colour. In the concentration camp everything was grey. But here in Holland the colours were vivid again. My eyes could not seem to get enough to satisfy them.

And the bed! Delightfully soft and clean with thick woollen blankets. One of the little nurses brought an extra pillow and tucked it under my swollen feet. I wanted to laugh and cry at the same time.

On a shelf was a row of books. Outside I heard the whistle of a boat on a canal and the merry sound of little children calling to one another as they skipped down the street. Far in the distance I heard the sound of a choir singing and then, oh, joy, the chimes of a carillon. I closed my eyes and tears wet my pillow. Only to those who have been in prison does freedom have such great meaning.

Later that afternoon one of the nurses took me up to her room where for the first time in many months I heard the sound of a radio. Gunther Ramin was playing a Bach trio. The organ tones flowed about and enveloped me. I sat on the floor beside a chair and sobbed, unashamedly. It was too much joy. I had rarely cried during all those months of suffering. Now I could not control myself. My life had been given back as a gift. Harmony, beauty, colours, and music. Only those who have suffered as I, and have returned, can fully understand what I mean. I knew my life had been given back for a purpose. I was no longer my own. This time I had been ransomed and released. I knew that God would soon be sending me out as a tramp for the Lord. But right now, He was letting me enjoy the luxury of thanksgiving. I was drinking from a fountain I knew would never run dry — the fountain of praise.

One of the first places I visited, after my release from the concentration camp, was the *Grote Kerk* in Haarlem. Since it was so close to where I had grown up in the Beje, I counted it as much of an old friend as I did the watch-maker's shop.

'May I show you through?' the old usher said as he met me at the door.

'If it is all right,' I said, 'I would like to be alone.'

He nodded, understandingly, and disappeared into the shadows of the sanctuary. I walked over the gravestones that formed the floor of the ancient building. My shoes made a strange, scraping sound that gave forth a hollow echo in the empty cathedral. I remembered the many times I had played here as a child.

My cousin Dot was my closest friend. She was the young-est daughter of my Uncle Arnold who was the previous usher — the caretaker — of the *Grote Kerk.*

Dot and I did everything together, but our favourite pas-time was to play hide-and-seek in the big church. There were many wonderful places to hide: pews, old doors giving en-trance to spiral staircases, and many closets. There was a world-famous pipe organ in the cathedral and sometimes when there was a concert, Uncle Arnold would allow members of his family to come into the church, sit on a wooden bench without a back and lean against the cold, moist stone wall to hear the magnificent music.

The cathedral was a symphony in grey tones during the

day, both inside and outside. In the evening, when the gas lamps were lit in the side transepts, we could see the pillars and ceilings pointing upwards, as the shadows danced about in a mysterious glow.

Only one place was absolutely 'off limits' as we played hide-and-seek. That was the old pulpit. We never went there, but for the rest — what a playground that old church was! When we shouted, the echo would ring from transept to transept and our laughter never, never seemed to be sacrilegious. Unlike some of the stern adults who sometimes frowned on our frolics, I had always thought that the laughter of the little children in an empty cathedral was the most beautiful of all hymns of praise. And so we grew up, knowing only a God who enjoyed our presence as we skipped, ran, and played through this building which was built for His glory.

One afternoon we played very late and before we knew it, the darkness of the cathedral swallowed us up. I looked around. Through the beautiful stained-glass windows I saw a little light coming in from the streets around. Only the silhouettes of the Gothic pillars stood out in the darkness as they reached upward and upward.

'Let's go home,' whispered Dot. 'I'm scared.'

I was not. Slowly I went to the usher's door that opened out to where Uncle Arnold lived. There was a Presence that comforted me, a deep peace in my heart. Even in the darkness, smelling the dust and dampness of the church building, I knew that the 'Light of the World' was present. Was the Lord preparing me for some time in the future when I would need to know that His light is victorious over all darkness?

It was forty-five years later. Betsie and I walked to the square where roll call was being held in the concentration camp. It was still early, before dawn. The head of our barracks was so cruel that she had sent us out into the very cold outdoors a full hour too early.

Betsie's hand was in mine. We went to the square by a different way from the rest of our barracks-mates. We were three as we walked with the Lord and talked with Him. Betsie spoke. Then I talked. Then the Lord spoke. How? I do not know. But both of us understood. It was the same Presence I had felt years before in the old cathedral in Haarlem.

The brilliant early morning stars were our only light. The cold winter air was so clear. We could faintly see the outlines of the barracks, the crematorium, the gas chamber, and the towers where the guards were standing with loaded machine guns.

'Isn't this a bit of heaven!' Betsie had said. 'And, Lord, this is a small foretaste. One day we will see You face-to-face, but thank You that even now You are giving us the joy of walking and talking with You.'

Heaven in the midst of hell. Light in the midst of darkness. What a security!

*Behold, God is my salvation; I will trust and
not be afraid: for the Lord JEHOVAH is my
strength and my song....*

Isaiah 12:2

4   A Song in the Night

The war was over. Even before I left the concentration
camp, I knew I would be busy helping those who had lost
their way. Now I found myself starting just such a work in
Bloemendaal. It was more than a home for the homeless; it
was a refuge for those who had lost their way spiritually as
well as physically.

Yet, because I had lived so close to death, looking it in the
face day after day, I often felt like a stranger among my
own people – many of whom looked upon money, honour
of men, and success as the important issues of life. Standing in front of a crematorium, knowing that any day
could be your day, gives one a different perspective on life.
The words of an old German motto kept flashing in my
mind:

What I spent, I had; what I saved, I lost; what I gave, I
have.

How well I understood the feeling of the artist who
painted the picture of the corpse of a once wealthy man and
entitled it, *Sic transit gloria mundi* — So passes the glory of

this world. The material things of this world no longer excited me — nor would they ever again.

It was during this time that I visited Haarlem, the town where I had spent more than fifty years of my life. It was late in the evening as I walked through the streets. Waiting before a traffic light, I had a strange feeling that the people should fall in line five by five, as in the concentration camp. Instead, they chatted about insignificant things and when the light changed, they moved on without anyone shouting at them.

Walking the streets that night, however, I felt growing in me a tremendous desire to tell all men, especially those in bondage to material things, of the One who can set us free from all prisons: Jesus.

It was after midnight when I finally made my way to the Barteljorisstraat. There were few streetlights but the moon and many stars were visible above the ancient rooftops of the familiar houses on the short street. I paused in front of the Beje on the corner of the small alley that came out in the midst of the street. I let my fingertips run across the door of the watchmaker's shop. Even though the Beje was no longer my home, it was still part of my heart. Little did I dream that one day it would be set aside as a museum to commemorate my family and the hiding place of those precious Jews who had been saved from certain death at the hands of the Nazis.

I stood alone in the darkness, allowing myself the sweet luxury of remembering. How often had I put the shutters before the show window. Through this door I had walked on my first day of school, almost fifty years ago. Oh, what an unwilling pupil I had been, crying in fear of leaving the dear old house whose warmth in winter had protected me, whose windows had kept out the rain and mist, whose cheery fire had welcomed me and others in the family each night after the dinner dishes had been put away. Yet my father, knowing my fear, took me by the hand and led me through this door and out into the world of learning, into an unknown world of teachers and classrooms.

Now Father was dead. Only My Heavenly Father remained. I ran my hand over the door, letting my fingers explore the cracks. It was no longer my hiding place. Others lived here now, and the world was my classroom, and my only security came in knowing that underneath were the Everlasting Arms. How thankful I was for my Heavenly Father's strong hand around mine.

I looked into the small alley. It was almost pitch dark. I strained my ears, and in the far off recesses of my heart, could imagine the voices of Father, Betsie, and the others. Had it been only a year ago? It seemed like centuries. 'What an honour,' Father had said, 'to give my life for God's chosen people, the Jews.'

I felt the wall with my hands, then gently pressed my face against the cold stones. No, I was not dreaming. It was reality. The old Beje, the old hiding place, was no longer mine. Ravensbruck had taught me much I needed to learn. My hiding place was now in Jesus alone. Even though I was wandering the streets at midnight in a town that used to be my home, but was now only a town, I knew the Presence of the Heavenly Father.

Suddenly the cathedral started to play its nostalgic chimes. Day and night through my lifetime I had heard the beautiful music from the *Grote Kerk*. It was not a dream, as I had often experienced in the concentration camp. It was real. I walked out of the shadows of the alley and made my way down the Barteljorisstraat to the *Grote Markt*. I paused to look at the cathedral which was silhouetted against the dark sky, framed into place by a million twinkling stars.

'Thank You, Jesus, that I am alive,' I said.

In my heart I heard Him reply, 'Lo, I am with you always, even unto the end of the world' (Matthew 28:20).

I stayed there for long minutes as the hands on the face of the great clock moved towards the hour. Then the chimes in the cathedral tower pealed forth once again, this time with the sounds of Luther's famous hymn 'A Mighty Fortress Is Our God'. I listened and heard myself singing the hymn, not in Dutch, but in German: *'Ein' feste Burg ist unser Gott.'*

'How like You, Lord,' I half-chuckled, 'that You would remind me of Your grace by letting me hear a German hymn.'

A policeman passed, looked at me, and spoke a friendly word.

I said, 'Good-night, Policeman. A mighty fortress is our God.'

I was free.

*By faith Abraham, when he was called to go
out into a place which he should after receive
for an inheritance, obeyed; and he went out,
not knowing whither he went.*

Hebrews 11:8

5 A Great Discovery

When my parents were married, many years ago, they
claimed Psalm 32:8 as their 'life verse', the promise which
they felt was God's assurance for them.

I will instruct thee and teach thee in the way which thou
shalt go: I will guide thee with mine eye.

Now that Father and Mother were gone, this promise
became the special directive for my life as well — God's
pledge to guide me in all my journeys. It was especially
needed as I set out for my first trip to America.

The war had only been over a short time, and many
Europeans wanted to go to America. However, few, if any,
wanted to go for the same reason I did — to carry the Gospel
as a missionary to the Americans. For all of us, however, it
was the same story when we applied for passage to America:
'It is impossible to obtain papers.'

I prayed, 'Lord, if it is Your will that I go to America,
then You must provide the necessary papers.'

I soon discovered that man's importunity is God's opportunity. He uses our problems as building materials for His

34

miracles. I began to understand that this was my first lesson in learning to trust Him completely, my first steps on the path to complete dependence on, and obedience to, His guidance. How much I had to learn!

At last all my papers were approved, except the final one — the most important one. I sat alone on a hard wooden bench in the hall of the Immigration Office in The Hague. Everyone coming out of the office warned those of us waiting in the hall, 'That fellow in there is as hard as flint. He passes no one.'

'Lord,' I prayed silently, 'I am willing to go or stay. It is up to You.'

'Hello, there! Don't we know each other?' It was the voice of a middle-aged woman standing in front of me. I looked up into her face, trying vainly to recognize her.

'You're Corrie ten Boom,' she laughed. 'I'm one of your cousins and this is Jan, my husband. I haven't seen you for years, and of course, Jan has never seen you since we were married only six years ago.'

'Are you trying to go to America, also?' I asked.

'Oh no,' she laughed. 'I'm visiting Jan. He has his office in this building.'

'Then perhaps you can help me,' I said, shaking his hand. I told him my story.

He was polite but said, 'I'm sorry. I would like to be of service to my brand-new cousin, but that's not my department. However, if you have trouble, ring me up.' He gave me his telephone number and we shook hands again as he left.

I continued to wait. The 'man of flint' left the office for coffee and a young clerk took his place. Then it was my turn.

'You had better wait until my boss returns,' the clerk said when I told him where I wanted to go and why.

35

My shoulders sagged. 'I cannot wait any longer. Won't you please call this number?' I handed him the card that Jan had handed me earlier.

I prayed while he placed the call. Moments later he hung up. 'All is arranged. I am approving your passport. You may make your trip to America.'

From there I travelled to Amsterdam to try to arrange passage on a ship of the Holland-America Line. However, another mountain loomed before me. The agent told me they would only put my name on the waiting list. 'We will notify you in about a year,' he said.

'A year! But I must go now.' The agent just shrugged his shoulders and returned to his work.

Disappointed, I returned to the square in the centre of the city. God had told me to go America — of that I was certain. All my papers were in order. God had seen to that also. Now it was up to Him to move this mountain. Glancing across the street I noticed a sign: AMERICAN EXPRESS COMPANY. Stepping into the office I enquired, 'Have you passenger accommodations on any of your freighters to America?'

The old clerk looked over his glasses and said, 'You may sail tomorrow, Madam, if your papers are in order.'

'Oh, tomorrow is too sudden,' I said, hardly believing what I heard. 'What about next week?'

'That, too, can be arranged,' he said. 'We don't have very many women your age who ship out on freighters. But if you are willing, so are we.'

Several weeks before I had met an American businessman who was visiting relatives in Holland. When I told him of my plans to visit American he tried to discourage me. 'It's not easy to make one's way in America,' he said.

'I believe you,' I told him. 'But God has directed me and I must obey.'

He then gave me two cheques, one small and one larger. 'If

you need it, use it,' he said. 'You can repay me later.' I tucked them away for safekeeping.

So I arrived in New York as a missionary to America. I was only allowed to bring in fifty dollars, and of course, I knew no one. However, I found my way to the YWCA where I found a room and a place to leave my bags.

I had the address of a group of Hebrew-Christian immigrants who were meeting in New York. I made a phone call and they invited me to come and speak. Since they were German, I could not use the English lectures I had prepared on board the ship, but had to speak to them in their native language. It was better perhaps, for my English was rather hard to understand.

At the end of the week after wandering around the city in a rather helpless daze, I went downstairs in the YWCA to pay my bill. The clerk looked at me sympathetically. 'I am sorry, but our accommodations are so restricted that we cannot allow you to stay here any longer. One week is our limit. Do you have a forwarding address?'

'Yes. I just don't know what it is, yet.'

'I don't understand,' she said, perplexed.

'God has another room for me,' I explained. 'He just hasn't told me what the address is. But I am not worried. He led me through Ravensbruck. He will surely see me through America as well.'

Suddenly the clerk remembered. 'By the way, a letter came for you.'

Strange, I thought, as she handed me the envelope. *How could I receive a letter? No one knows where I am staying.* But there it was. I read it hurriedly and then turned to the clerk. 'My forwarding address will be this house on 190th Street.'

'But why didn't you tell me that before?' she asked.

'I didn't know. It was in this letter. A woman that I do not know writes, "I heard you speak to the Jewish congregation. I am aware that it is almost impossible to get a room in New York City. My son happens to be in Europe, so you are welcome to use his room as long as you are in New York." '

The lady at the desk was more amazed than I. However, I reasoned, perhaps she had not experienced miracles before.

I rode the subway to 190th Street. The house at the address was a large, multistoried building occupied by many families. I found the correct apartment at the end of a hall, but no one was home. Certainly my hostess did not expect her invitation to be an eleventh-hour answer to my problem. I arranged myself among my suitcases on the floor, and leaning against the wall, soon began to drift off to sleep.

In those last moments before sleep took over, my mind drifted back to Ravensbruck. I could feel Betsie's bony hand touching my face. It was pitch black in Barracks 28 where seven hundred other prisoners were asleep. Each day hundreds of women died and their bodies were fed to the ovens. Betsie had grown so weak, and we both knew that death was always moments away.

'Are you awake, Corrie?' Her weak voice sounded so far away.

'Yes, you wakened me.'

'I had to. I need to tell you what God has said to me.'

'Shhh. We hinder the sleep of the girls around us. Let us lie with our faces toward each other.'

The cot was so small. We could only lie like spoons in a box, our knees bumping against the knees of the other. We used our two coats as covers along with the thin black blanket provided by the Nazis.

I pulled the coat over our heads so we could whisper and not be heard. 'God showed me,' Betsie said, 'that after the war we must give to the Germans that which they now try to take away from us: our love for Jesus.'

Betsie's breath was coming in short gasps. She was so weak, her body wasted away until there was nothing but her thin skin stretched over brittle bones. 'Oh, Betsie,' I exclaimed, 'you mean if we live we will have to return to Germany?'

Betsie patted my hand under the blanket. 'Corrie, there is so much bitterness. We must tell them that the Holy Spirit will fill their hearts with God's love.'

I remembered Romans 5:5. Only that morning some of the women in the barracks had huddled with us in the corner while I read from our precious Bible. But I shuddered. Germany. If I were ever released from this horrible place could I ever return to Germany?

Betsie's weak voice whispered on. 'This concentration camp here at Ravensbruck has been used to destroy many, many lives. There are many other such camps throughout Germany. After the war they will not have use for them anymore. I have prayed that the Lord will give us one in Germany. We will use it to build up lives.'

No, I thought. *I will return to my simple job as a watchmaker in Holland and never again set my boot across the border.*

Betsie's voice was quivering so I could barely understand her. 'The Germans are the most wounded of all the people in the world. Think of that young girl guard who swore in such filthy language yesterday. She was only seventeen or eighteen years old, but did you see how she was beating that poor old woman with a whip? What a job there is to do after the war.'

I found a place where I could put my hand. It was such a stupid problem, I thought, yet it was a small cot and it was difficult to position my hands and arms. My hand rested on

Betsie's left side, just on her heart. I felt her ribs — only skin and bones. How long would she be able to live? Her heart was fluttering inside the rib cage like a dying bird, as though it would stop any moment.

I rested and thought. How close to God's heart was Betsie. Only God could see in such circumstances the possibility for ministry in the future — ministry to those who even now were preparing to kill us. Most of all, to see in such a place as Ravensbruck an opportunity to bless and build up the lives of our enemies. Yes, only the Lord Jesus could have given Betsie such a vision.

'Must we live with them in Germany?' I whispered.

'For a while,' Betsie answered. 'Then we will travel the whole world bringing the Gospel to all — our friends as well as our enemies.'

'To *all* the world? But that will take much money.'

'Yes, but God will provide,' Betsie said. 'We must do nothing else but bring the Gospel and He will take care of us. After all, He owns the cattle on a thousand hills. If we need money we will just ask the Father to sell a few cows.'

I was beginning to catch the vision. 'What a privilege,' I said softly, 'to travel the world and be used by the Lord Jesus.'

But Betsie did not answer. She had fallen asleep. Three days later she was dead.

Going to bed the night after Betsie died was one of the most difficult tasks of my life. The one electric light bulb was screwed into the ceiling toward the front of the room. Only a feeble ray reached my narrow cot. I lay in the semi-darkness — thinking — remembering — trying to reconstruct Betsie's vision.

There was a shuffle of feet near my bed and I looked up. A Russian woman, thin and gaunt, was shuffling down the aisle between the beds looking for a place to sleep. The Russians were not received kindly and everyone turned away. As she neared me I saw the hunted look in her eyes. How awful to be in prison and not have even a place to sleep!

Betsie's place beside me was vacant. I motioned to the woman and threw back the blanket for her. She crept in, gratefully, and stetched out beside me. We were sharing the same pillow and with our faces so close I wanted to speak. But I did not know her language.

'*Jesoes Christoes?*' I asked softly.

'Oh!' she exclaimed. Quickly making the sign of the cross, she threw her arms about me and kissed me.

She who had been my sister for fifty-two years, with whom I had shared so much of weal and woe, had left me. A Russian woman now claimed my love. And there would be others, too, who would be my sisters and brothers in Christ all across the world.

I was awakened by a gentle hand shaking my shoulder. It was after midnight and I realized I had fallen asleep in the midst of my suitcases, sitting on the floor, and leaning against the wall of the hallway.

'Come,' my new friend said softly as she opened the door, 'the floor is no place for a child of the King.' I rose from my cramped, huddled position and entered her apartment. I was her guest for the next five weeks.

As the weeks passed, however, I realized I was running out of money. Jan ten Have (the publisher of my little book in Holland) was visiting New York. He helped me as much as he could, and I spent most of my time looking up addresses given me in Holland. The Americans were polite and some of them were interested, but none wanted me to come to speak. They were all busy with their own things. Some even said I should have stayed in Holland.

As the weeks slipped by, I found more and more resistance to my ministry. No one was interested in a middle-aged spinster woman from Holland who wanted to preach. 'Why did you come to America?' people began to ask.

'God directed me. All I could do was obey.'

'That's nonsense,' they answered. 'There is no such thing as direct guidance from God. Experience proves we must use our common sense. If you are here and out of money, then it is your fault, not God's.'

I tried to argue back in God's defence. 'But God's guidance is even more important than common sense. I am certain He told me to bring His message to America. I can declare that the deepest darkness is outshone by the light of Jesus.'

'We have ministers to tell us such things,' was the reply.

'Certainly, but I can tell from my experience in a concentration camp that what such ministers say is true.'

'It would have been better for you to have remained in Holland. We don't need any more preachers. Too many Europeans come to America. They should be stopped.'

I was growing discouraged. Perhaps the Americans were right. Perhaps I should return to Holland and go back to my job as a watchmaker. My money was gone, and all that remained was the second cheque given me by the American businessman. Yet I was hesitant to cash it without his approval. I found his address and arrived in an imposing business office in Manhattan. Only this time his face was not as friendly as it had been in Holland.

'Do you mind if I cash your second cheque?' I asked.

'How do I know if you can return the money?' he asked. 'You've been in America five weeks and have found there is no work. I think it would be better if you simply returned the cheque.'

42

Mustering all my courage I said, 'I am sure God has work for me here. I am in His will, and will somehow return all your money.'

He snorted, tore up the cheque and then wrote out another — for a much smaller amount.

I was embarrassed and humbled. I had money in Holland — a balance left from my first book and a small income from the business I had sold. But these funds could not be brought to America. I returned to my room and closed the door. It was time for a long consultation with my Heavenly Father.

Kneeling beside the bed I prayed, 'Father, You must help me out. If I must borrow money to return to Holland people will say, "There, you see, the promises of the Bible are not real. Direct guidance does not exist." Father, for Your honour's sake. You must help me out.'

I fell weeping across the bed. Then, slowly, like a deep realization that dawns in a person's heart, the answer came: 'Do not worry about My honour. I will take care of that. In days to come you will give thanks for these days in New York.'

A great ocean separated me from my homeland. I had no money. Nobody wanted to hear my lectures. All I had was an inner word from God that He was guiding me. Was it enough? All I could do was press on — and on — and on — for His Name's sake.

Before going to sleep I opened my Bible, my constant companion. My eyes fell on a verse from the Psalms, 'The Lord taketh pleasure . . . in those that hope in His mercy' (147:11). It was a thin web — a tiny filament — stretching from heaven to my little room on 190th Street in New York. I fell asleep holding on to it with all my strength.

The next day I attended a Dutch service in a New York church. Dr. Barkay Wolf was the speaker and many Hollanders were present, meeting afterward for coffee in the vestry. The Reverend Burggraaff, who had baptized our Canadian-born princess, was presented to me.

'ten Boom,' he mused when he heard my name. 'I often tell the story of a nurse by that name. She experienced a miracle in a concentration camp with a bottle of vitamins that never ran out. I tell it to prove that God still performs miracles today, as in Bible times. Do you happen to know that nurse? Is she related to you?'

I felt joy springing in my heart. 'She is not a nurse,' I replied. 'She is a watchmaker. And you are looking at her. It was I who had that experience in 1944.'

'Then you must come with me to Staten Island and tell your story to my congregation,' he exclaimed.

I spent the next five days in this pleasant parsonage with Rev. and Mrs. Burggraaff. What a joy to eat good Dutch food again. I had been trying to find out how long one could exist on Nedick's ten-cent breakfast which consisted of a cup of coffee, a doughnut, and a small glass of orange juice, eaten while standing at a counter. Now God was re-supplying me, not only with food, but with new hope. I could see that the Lord does take pleasure in those that hope in His mercy!

A week later I returned to Manhattan. Walking down the street I saw a church with a notice on the door. Drawing closer I saw it was an invitation to attend the Lord's Supper next Sunday morning, Easter.

Following the service, the minister gave me the address of Irving Harris, the editor of a Christian magazine called *The Evangel*. He encouraged me to go by and see him.

I did. In fact, the very next morning I went up to his office and talked to him. 'I know I am walking in the way God has led me,' I told him, 'but so many declare there is no such thing as direct guidance.'

'Pay no attention to them,' Mr. Harris advised. 'The Bible contains many promises that God will lead those who obey Him. Have you ever heard of a good shepherd who does not lead his sheep?'

Mr. Harris asked if I had any material which he might use in his magazine. I gave him a copy of one of my lectures and told him to use as much as he could.

'There is one drawback,' he explained. 'We cannot pay. This paper exists only to spread the Gospel, not for financial profit.'

'Wonderful!' I exclaimed. 'I am in the presence of an American who sees money in its proper perspective.'

Mr. Harris gave me a name and address in Washington, D.C. He strongly urged me to make an appointment and go down to see Mr. Abraham Vereide. I knew nothing of Mr. Vereide at the time, although I have since discovered he was one of the great Christian leaders of America. I was suspicious, afraid I was being shrugged off again. But I felt I could trust Mr. Harris and followed through, taking a chance and making a phone call to Washington.

Mr. Vereide received me graciously, inviting me to Washington as his guest. At dinner three other guests were present, all professors who plied me with questions throughout the evening. I felt like a schoolgirl who had been invited out by her headmistress. My English was crude and my mistakes seemed more glaring than ever before. How could I compete with such learned men?

The next afternoon, however, I was asked to address a group of women. They asked specifically that I share my prison experiences with them. This time I felt at home. Certainly I could tell them what the Lord had done in my life.

They received me warmly — enthusiastically in fact. 'Corrie,' one of the ladies said afterwards, 'this is your message. Share it wherever you go.' She then handed me a cheque that enabled me to return all the money I had borrowed in New York.

Suddenly the tables were turned. Instead of no work, I had to guard against overwork. Abraham Vereide's recommendation brought in calls from everyplace, asking me to come and share my testimony. The calls came from villages and towns, as well as from the big cities. I spoke in churches, universities, schools, and clubs. For almost ten months I travelled America, everywhere telling the story that Jesus Christ is reality, even in darkest days. I told them that He is the answer to all the problems in the hearts of men and nations. I knew it was so, because of what He had done for me.

As the year drew to a close I began to sense God wanted me to return to Europe. I was homesick for Holland, but this time I felt Him leading me in another direction — Germany. The one land I dreaded.

When I left the German concentration camp I said, 'I'll go anywhere God sends me, but I hope never to Germany.' Now I understand that was a statement of disobedience. F. B. Meyer said, 'God does not fill with His Holy Spirit those who believe in the fullness of the Spirit, or those who desire Him, but those who obey Him.' More than anything I desired to be filled with God's Spirit. I knew I had no choice but to go to Germany.

I will sing of the mercies of the Lord for ever:
with my mouth will I make known they faith-
fulness to all generations.

Psalms 89:1

6 Music From Broken Chords

The Germans had lost face in defeat. Their homes had been destroyed and when they heard the enormity of Hitler's crimes (which many Germans knew nothing about) they were filled with despair. As they returned to their Fatherland they felt they had nothing to live for.

Friends in Darmstadt helped me rent a former concentration camp to use as a home for displaced persons. It was not big, but there was room for about one hundred and sixty refugees and soon it was full with a long waiting list. I worked closely with the refugees programme of the Lutheran Church ('*das Evangelische Hilfswerk*') in the Darmstadt camp. Barbed wire disappeared. Flowers, light-coloured paint and God's love in the hearts of the people changed a cruel camp into a refuge where people would find the way back to life again.

Marienschwestern, the Lutheran Sisterhood of Mary, whose members had dedicated their lives to serving the Lord and spiritually hungry people, assisted with the children's and women's work. Pastors and members of different churches helped by building homes. I was travelling and helping raise money for the work.

The camp was crowded. Some rooms were jammed with several families. Noise and bedlam were everywhere as families, many without men because they had been killed in the war, tried to carry on the most basic forms of living. Often I would walk through the camp talking with the lonely, defeated people and trying to bring them hope and cheer.

One afternoon I spotted an elderly woman huddled in the corner of a big room. She was obviously new to the camp. She had been put in the big room along with three other families and told she could set up housekeeping in the corner. There she crouched, like a whipped child, her faded, worn dress pulled tightly around her frail, wasted body. I could sense she was distressed by the bedlam of all the crying children, but most of all defeated by life itself.

I went to her, sat beside her on the floor, and asked who she was. I learned she had been a professor of music at the Dresden Conservatory before the war. Now she had nothing.

I asked her to tell me about her life, knowing that sometimes it helps just to have someone willing to listen. She told me that a minister in a nearby town had given her permission to play his piano. She had also learned of several farmers' children nearby who wanted to receive music lessons. But the minister's home was miles away and the only way to get there was on foot. It all seemed so hopeless.

'You were a professor of piano?' I asked excitedly. 'I am a great lover of Germany's master musician, Johann Sebastian Bach.'

For an instant her eyes lighted up. 'Would you care to accompany me to the minister's home?' she asked with great dignity. 'I would be most happy to play for you.'

It was a great privilege, and even though we had to walk many miles, I sensed God was doing something special.

She seated herself at the battered piano. I looked at the

48

instrument. Even though it had been saved from the bombing it had not been protected from the rain. The strings were exposed through the warped frame and I could see they were rusted. Some were broken and curled around the others. The pedals had long been broken off and the keyboard was almost entirely without ivory. If any of the notes played it would be a miracle.

Looking up the old woman said, 'What would you like me to play?'

Silently I prayed, knowing that failure at this moment could crush her forever. Then, to my own amazement, I heard myself saying, 'Would you please play the "Chromatic Phantasy" of Bach?'

I was aghast. Why had I picked one of the most difficult of all piano pieces for this old woman to play on such a ruined instrument? Yet the moment I said it, I saw a light flicker behind her eyes and a slight, knowing smile played across her tired face. She nodded, and with great finesse, put her fingers on the broken keyboard.

I could hardly believe my ears. From that damp, battered old piano flowed the beautiful music of Bach as her skilled fingers raced up and down the broken, chipped keys. Tears came to my eyes and ran down my cheeks as I thought of wounded Germany, left with only the remnants of the past, still able to play beautiful music. Such a nation will survive to create again, I thought.

As the notes of Bach faded from the air the words of an old Gospel song, written by the blind composer Fanny J. Crosby, came to mind:

Down in the human heart, crush'd by the tempter,
Feelings lie buried that grace can restore;
Touched by a loving heart, wakened by kindness
Chords that were broken will vibrate once more.

As we walked back to the former concentration camp my companion had a new spring in her step. 'It has been many years since I played the "Chromatic Phantasy",' she said. 'Once I was a concert pianist and many of my pupils are now outstanding musicians. I had a beautiful home in Dresden that was destroyed by the bombs. I had to flee and was not able to take one thing with me.'

'Oh, no, you are wrong,' I said. 'You took with you your most prized possession.'

'And what is that?' she asked, shocked.

'Your music. For that which is in your heart can never be taken from you.'

Then I told her of what I had learned in Ravensbruck, of Betsie's vision, and that God's love still stands when all else has fallen. 'In the concentration camp they took all we had, even made us stand naked for hours at a time without rest, but they could not take Jesus from my heart. Ask Jesus to come into your life. He will give you riches no man can take away from you.'

We returned to the camp in silence, but I knew the Holy Spirit was pricking her heart, reminding her of the things that man cannot snatch from us. Soon it was time for me to leave the camp and move on to other fields. The day I left she was sitting in that same corner of the room. A boy was playing his mouth organ, a baby was crying, there were the sounds of shouts and the pounding of a hammer against a wooden crate. The room was full of discord and disharmonic noises, but her eyes were closed and there was a faint smile on her face. I knew God had given her something that no one could ever take from her — ever again.

After the war, Germany was filled with wounds and scars — not all of them on the surface. In one tiny cubicle in the camp at Darmstadt, I found a German lawyer. He was sitting miserably in a wheelchair, the stumps of his legs poking out from under a lap blanket. He was filled with bitterness, hatred, and self-pity. He told me he had once been an active member of his Lutheran church and as a boy had rung the church bell in the village where he lived. Now the horrible injustice of war had taken his legs, and he was bitter against God and man.

I felt attracted to him since some of his experiences were similar to mine. One morning I made a special trip to his room to tell him something of my life.

I found him sitting in his wheelchair, staring at a blank wall. His face was grey, his eyes lifeless. I never was one for introductions so I got right to the point of my visit.

'The only way to get rid of bitterness is to surrender it,' I said.

He turned slowly and looked at me. 'What do you know about bitterness?' he asked. 'You still have your legs.'

'Let me tell you a story,' I said. 'In Holland, during the war, a man came to me begging me to help him liberate his wife. I felt compassion for him and gave him all my money. I also convinced my friends to do the same. But the man was a quisling, a traitor. The only reason he came to me was to trap me so he could have me arrested. Not only did he betray me, but he betrayed my entire family and friends. We were all sent to prison where three members of my family died. You ask me about bitterness and hatred. You only hate circumstances, but I hated a man. Sitting in the prison in my homeland, waiting to be transferred to a concentration camp in Germany, hatred and bitterness filled my heart. I wanted that man to die. I know what it is like to hate. That is why I can understand you.'

The lawyer turned his chair to face me. He was listening. 'So you have hated also. What do you suggest I do about my hate?'

'What I have to say is of no importance. Let me tell you what the Son of God had to say. "For if ye forgive men their trespasses, your Heavenly Father will also forgive you. But if ye forgive not men their trespasses, neither will your Father forgive your trespasses." (*See* Matthew 6:14, 15.) If we forgive other people, our hearts are made fit to receive forgiveness.'

The lawyer shifted uneasily in his wheelchair. I could see the muscles in his neck stand out as he pushed with his hands to change position. 'When we repent,' I continued, 'God forgives us and cleanses us. That is what I did, believing that if I confessed my sin God would be faithful and just to cleanse my sin and forgive me from all unrighteousness.'

The lawyer looked at me and shook his head. 'That is easy to say, but my hatred is too deep to have it washed away.'

'No deeper than mine,' I said. 'Yet when I confessed it, not only did Jesus take it away, He filled me with love — even the ability to love my enemy.'

'You mean you actually loved the man who betrayed you and who was responsible for the death of your family?'

I nodded. 'After the war, when that man was sentenced to death, I corresponded with him and God used me to show him the way of salvation before he was executed.'

The lawyer shook his head. 'What a miracle! What a miracle! You mean Jesus can do that to a person? I shall have to give this much thought.'

Since I have learned not to push a person beyond where God has left him, I bade my friend good-bye and returned to my room.

A year later I was in Darmstadt again. My friends had given this man a car with special fixtures so he could drive without legs. He met me at the train station to bring me to

52

the camp. As I got in the car, he laughed at my startled look.

'You taught me that Jesus is victor,' he said. 'Now surely you are not afraid to drive with a man who has no legs.'

'You are right,' I answered. 'I shall not be afraid. I am so glad to see you again. How are you?'

'Fine. I must tell you at the very beginning that I have surrendered my bitterness to God. I repented and the Lord did just as you said. He forgave me and filled my heart with His love. Now I am working in the refugee camp and am praising God that He can use even a legless man if he is surrendered.'

He paused, and then continued. 'But there is something I must know. After you forgave your enemies, was it settled once and for all?'

'Oh no,' I answered. 'Just this month I had a sad experience with friends who behaved like enemies. They promised something but did not keep their promise. In fact, they took great advantage of me. However, I surrendered my bitterness to the Lord, asked forgiveness and He took it away.'

We were bouncing over a bumpy road but the lawyer was more intent on me than his driving. 'Was the bitterness gone for good, then?'

'No, just the next night, at four o'clock, I awoke and my heart was filled with bitterness again. I thought, *How could my dear friend behave as she did?* Again I brought it to the Lord. He filled my heart with His love. But the next night it came back again. I was so discouraged. God had used me often to help people to love their enemies, and I could always give my testimony about what He had done in my life; but now I felt defeated.

'Then I remembered Ephesians 6:10–20 where Paul describes the "armour of God". He said that even after you have come to a standstill, still stand your ground. I was at a standstill, so I decided to stand my ground and the bitterness and resentment fell away before me.

'Corrie ten Boom without the Lord Jesus cannot be victorious. I need the Lord every moment. And I have learned that I am absolutely dependent on Him. Because of this He has made me rich.'

We were just arriving at the refugee camp and my lawyer friend parked before the building, turned off the motor, and looked at me with a grin. 'I am glad to hear that,' he said. 'For sometimes my old bitterness returns. Now I shall just stand my ground, claim the victory of Jesus over fear and resentment, and love even when I don't want to.'

My friend had learned well the secret of victory. It comes through obedience.

> ... we feel this warm love everywhere within
> us because God has given us the Holy Spirit to
> fill our hearts with his love.
>
> Romans 5:5 LB

7 Love Your Enemy

It was in a church in Munich that I saw him — a balding, heavy-set man in a grey overcoat, a brown felt hat clutched between his hands. People were filing out of the basement room where I had just spoken, moving along the rows of wooden chairs to the door at the rear. It was 1947 and I had come from Holland to defeated Germany with the message that God forgives.

It was the truth they needed most to hear in that bitter, bombed-out land, and I gave them my favourite mental picture. Maybe because the sea is never far from a Hollander's mind, I liked to think that that's where forgiven sins were thrown. 'When we confess our sins,' I said, 'God casts them into the deepest ocean, gone forever. And even though I cannot find a Scripture for it, I believe God then places a sign out there that says, NO FISHING ALLOWED.'

The solemn faces stared back at me, not quite daring to believe. There were never questions after a talk in Germany in 1947. People stood up in silence, in silence collected their wraps, in silence left the room.

And that's when I saw him, working his way forward against the others. One moment I saw the overcoat and the brown hat; the next, a blue uniform and a visored cap with its skull and crossbones. It came back with a rush: the huge room with its harsh overhead lights; the pathetic pile of dresses and shoes in the centre of the floor; the shame of walking naked past this man. I could see my sister's frail form ahead of me, ribs sharp beneath the parchment skin. *Betsie, how thin you were!*

The place was Ravensbruck and the man who was making his way forward had been a guard — one of the most cruel guards.

Now he was in front of me, hand thrust out: 'A fine message, Fraulein! How good it is to know that, as you say, all our sins are at the bottom of the sea!'

And I, who had spoken so glibly of forgiveness, fumbled in my pocketbook rather than take that hand. He would not remember me, of course — how could he remember one prisoner among those thousands of women?

But I remembered him and the leather crop swinging from his belt. I was face-to-face with one of my captors and my blood seemed to freeze.

'You mentioned Ravensbruck in your talk,' he was saying. 'I was a guard there.' No, he did not remember me.

'But since that time,' he went on, 'I have become a Christian. I know that God has forgiven me for the cruel things I did there, but I would like to hear it from your lips as well. Fraulein,' — again the hand came out — 'will you forgive me?'

And I stood there — I whose sins had again and again to be forgiven — and could not forgive. Betsie had died in that place — could he erase her slow terrible death simply for the asking?

It could not have been many seconds that he stood there — hand held out — but to me it seemed hours as I wrestled with the most difficult thing I had ever had to do.

56

For I had to do it — I knew that. The message that God forgives has a prior condition: that we forgive those who have injured us. 'If you do not forgive men their trespasses,' Jesus says, 'neither will your Father in heaven forgive your trespasses.'

I knew it not only as a commandment of God, but as a daily experience. Since the end of the war I had had a home in Holland for victims of Nazi brutality. Those who were able to forgive their former enemies were able also to return to the outside world and rebuild their lives, no matter what the physical scars. Those who nursed their bitterness remained invalids. It was as simple and as horrible as that.

And still I stood there with the coldness clutching my heart. But forgiveness is not an emotion — I knew that too. Forgiveness is an act of the will, and the will can function regardless of the temperature of the heart. 'Jesus, help me!' I prayed silently. 'I can lift my hand. I can do that much. You supply the feeling.'

And so woodenly, mechanically, I thrust my hand into the one stretched out to me. And as I did, an incredible thing took place. The current started in my shoulder, raced down my arm, sprang into our joined hands. And then this healing warmth seemed to flood my whole being, bringing tears to my eyes.

'I forgive you, brother!' I cried. 'With all my heart.'

For a long moment we grasped each other's hands, the former guard and the former prisoner. I had never known God's love so intensely as I did then. But even so, I realized it was not my love. I had tried, and did not have the power. It was the power of the Holy Spirit as recorded in Romans 5:5, '. . . because the love of God is shed abroad in our hearts by the Holy Ghost which is given unto us.'

(Reprinted by permission from GUIDEPOSTS MAGAZINE, Copyright 1972 by Guideposts Associates, Inc., Carmel, New York 10512.)

*And Jesus being full of the Holy Ghost re-
turned from Jordan, and was led by the Spirit into
the wilderness.... And Jesus returned in the
power of the Spirit into Galilee: and there went
out a fame of him through all the region round
about.*

Luke 4:1, 14

8 In the Power of the Spirit

As I stood in the railroad station in Basel, Switzerland, waiting for my luggage, I suddenly realized that I did not know
where I was supposed to go. For ten years, after my release
from prison, I had been travelling all over the world at the
direction of God. Many times I did not know why I was to go
to a certain place until I arrived. It had become almost
second nature not to make my plans and then ask for God's
signature. Rather, I had learned to wait for God's plan and
then write my name on the schedule.

But this time was different. Suddenly I was in Basel and
had no idea why, or whom I was to contact. Besides, I was
tired. Sleeping each night in a different bed and always living
out of a suitcase had worn me down. I felt a sensation of
panic in my heart and sat down, trying to remember to
whom I was going. At sixty-three years of age could it be
that I was so overworked that I was losing my memory? Or
even worse, had God withdrawn His conscious Presence
from me and was letting me walk alone for a season?

Inside my suitcase I found an address. It had no meaning
to me but it was all I had to go on. I took a taxi to the place
but the people at that address were complete strangers and

58

had never heard of me. By now I was desperate — and a little bit frightened.

The people told me of another man I might contact. Perhaps he would know who I was and why I had come to Basel. I took another taxi but this gentleman, too, was unfamiliar with my work.

For ten years the Lord had guided me step-by-step. At no time had I been confused or afraid. Now I was both — unable to recognize the Presence of God. Surely He was still guiding me, but like the pilot who flies into the clouds, I was now having to rely on instruments rather than sight. I decided to turn around and go back home to Holland, there to await further orders.

Because of a severe storm the planes were not flying. I had to travel by train. Arriving at Haarlem, I started towards the phone near the station to call Zonneduin, the house where I was to stay in the outskirts of the city in Bloemendaal.

But on the way to the phone booth I slipped on the wet pavement and before I knew it I was sprawled in the street. A sharp pain shot through my hip and I was unable to stand.

'Oh, Lord,' I prayed, 'lay Your hand on my hip and take away this horrible pain.'

Instantly the pain disappeared, but I was still unable to get up. Kind people assisted me to a taxi where a policeman asked if he could help.

'What is your name?' he asked.

'Corrie ten Boom.'

He looked surprised and questioned me further. 'Are you a member of the family of that name whom we arrested about ten years ago?'

'That is right.'

During the war many of the good Dutch policemen had been in the service of the Gestapo, remaining there for the express purpose of helping political prisoners. This man had been on duty that day my family was arrested.

'I am so sorry about your accident,' he said sympathetically, 'but I am glad to see you again. I will never forget that night in the police station. You were all sitting or lying on the floor of the station. Your old father was there with all his children and many of your friends. I have often told my colleagues that there was an atmosphere of peace and joy in our station that night, as if you were going to a feast instead of prison and death.'

He paused and looked at me kindly as if trying to remember my face. 'Your father said before he tried to sleep, "Let us pray together." And then he read Psalm 91.'

'You remember!' I exclaimed. After ten years that policeman had remembered which psalm my father had read.

For a fleeting moment, sitting in that old taxi on a Haarlem street while the rain pelted the roof, I allowed myself that pain of looking backwards. It was in this same city that we had been arrested. In fact, the prison was only a short distance from where I was now sitting. That was the last time our family had been together. Within ten days Father was dead. Then later Betsie. All gone. Now, ten years later this policeman still remembered.

He that dwelleth in the secret place of the most High shall abide under the shadow of the Almighty.

verse 1

Now the message was clear. Although there was no light to guide me, I was still in God's will. Actually, when one is abiding under the shadow of the Almighty there will be no light, but that is only because God's Presence is so near.

I leaned back in the seat. 'Dear God, when this shadow came over me I thought You had departed. Now I understand it was because You were drawing closer. I eagerly await whatever You have planned for me.'

Eager I was, but not so patient. An X-ray showed my hip was not broken, only badly bruised. The doctor said I would have to remain in bed for several weeks for it to heal. I was taken from the clinic to Zonneduin where I was put to bed, unable to move or turn over without the help of a nurse.

I was a very impatient patient. I had only five days to get to a student conference in Germany and as the days slipped by and I realized my hip was not healing fast enough to make the conference, I grew irritable.

'Is there not a Christian in all Haarlem who can pray for me to be healed?' I asked.

My friends sent for a particular minister in the city who was known to have laid hands on the sick for healing. That same afternoon he came to my room.

Standing beside my bed he said, 'Is there any unconfessed sin in your life?'

What an odd question, I thought. I understood he had agreed to come and pray for my healing, but was it his job to get so personal about my sins and attitudes? However, I did not have far to look. My impatience and demanding attitude which I had displayed towards my nurse had been wrong — very wrong. I asked her to come to the room and I repented of my sin, asking both her and God to forgive me.

Satisfied, this gentle man then reached over and laid his hands on my head. Only the year before my sister Nollie had died. Ever since my heart had been broken with mourning. I had the feeling of being left all alone and knew that the insecurity which I had experienced had contributed to my being here in this bed, rather than in Germany with the students. Yet as this tall, handsome man laid his hands on me and prayed, I felt a great stream of power flowing through me. Such great joy. The mourning left and I wanted to sing with David:

Thou hast turned for me my mourning into dancing: thou has put off my sackcloth, and girded me with gladness.

Psalms 30:11

I felt the Presence of the Lord Jesus all around me and felt His love flowing through me and over me as if I were being immersed in an ocean of grace. My joy became so intense that I finally prayed, 'No more, Lord, no more.' My heart felt it was about to burst, so great was the joy. I knew it was that wonderful experience promised by Jesus — the Baptism in the Holy Spirit.

I looked at the man who had prayed for me. 'Can I walk now?' I asked.

He smiled. 'I do not know. All I know is you asked for a cupful and God gave you an ocean.'

Ten days later I was on my way to Germany, late, but still filled with joy overflowing. Only after I arrived did I realize why God chose this particular time to fill me with His Holy Spirit. For in Germany, for the first time, I came face-to-face with many people who were demonized. Had I gone in my own power I would have been consumed. Now, going in the power of the Holy Spirit, God was able to work much deliverance through me as we commanded demons to be cast out in the Name of the Lord Jesus Christ.

Jesus specifically warned His followers not to try to minister in His Name without His power. As I found out from my experience in Basel, trying to do the Lord's work in your own strength is the most confusing, exhausting, and tedious of all work. But when you are filled with the Holy Spirit, then the ministry of Jesus just flows out of you.

It was the beginning of a new spiritual blessing that each

day brings me into a closer walk with the Lord Jesus. Now, whether I am walking in the bright light of His Presence, or abiding under the *shadow* of the Almighty, I know that He is not only with me, He is in me.

... greater is he that is in you, than he that is in the world.

1 John 4:4

9   Conny

After twelve years of travelling alone, someone joined me in
my worldwide travels. The Lord saw and supplied my need
in the person of Conny van Hoogstraten, a beautiful, young,
Dutch woman who became my first constant travelling companion. I met her on one of my visits to England. We
worked well as a team (not to say we did not have
difficulties — as always happens when people work so close
together). However, those hard moments were used to bring
us closer to Jesus as we learned to walk in the light with each
other. Yes, 1 John 1:7–9 became a reality, and the Lord used
Conny in the lives of countless people all over the world to
show and teach them the joy of walking in the light.

We laughed much together for the Lord had given Conny
an infectious sense of humour and a happy laughter. One of
Conny's special gifts was the ability to change a house into a
home. People always found an open door and quickly
became friends. We were both so different but the Lord
moulded us into a team fit to do His work. I will never forget
the day, now almost eight years ago, that Conny told me of
the someone else who had come into her life and that we
would have to pray for a new partner. That was one of those

very difficult days and the best thing I could do was to go for a long walk. I experienced more than ever before that I was so dependent upon Conny and that I loved her like a sister. I could not understand the Lord's purpose, but during that walk I surrendered Conny to the Lord, and I also surrendered myself in a new way and entrusted my whole being to Him who knew best. Conny was in good hands so why not trust Him for the future? Those last years together were so different from all other years.

In that final year together, the Lord made it clear to me to go to Viet Nam. Conny and I talked it over and Conny shared with me that her fiancé was not in favour of her going there so we had to look around for someone else. It was early spring and I happened to meet a good brother in the Lord who shared that he had been called to go to Viet Nam also. I rejoiced and thanked the Lord as we made plans to go together. The young man was Brother Andrew and he proved to be a very good travelling companion. In Viet Nam, the Lord gave me a very nice nurse who worked with the W.E.C. and she took care of me when I travelled while Brother Andrew was away on other trips to very dangerous places.

I will never forget the tremendous needs I saw in the hospitals and other places I visited, but instead of taking all those needs to Jesus, I kept them in my heavy and overburdened heart. How silly I could be! With that heavy heart and aching body I had to go on to Indonesia. Oh, the Lord worked in spite of me, and the people were very kind to me and helped me in many ways, but the happiest moment came when we landed in Amsterdam. We quickly drove to Soestdijk where a very dear friend, Elisabeth van Heemstra (who was working in Jerusalem at that time) had made her apartment available to me. That was a great gift from the Lord! I had no place I could really call home but now I had one — and what a haven it was! Beautiful surroundings in a quiet section of town. There Conny and I spent our last months together and it was a precious time. Conny was busy with marriage preparations and the new house she and her husband would move into. Many old-time friends came by to say hello. We talked and prayed much and we trusted that the Lord would supply a new partner before Conny's marriage.

How marvellous are His ways! The Lord answered our prayers and gave me another Dutch companion. Her name is Ellen de Kroon, a registered nurse, who loves the Lord very much. I will never forget the first time Ellen visited me. Conny and her fiancé were there also. It was a nice day in June and we decided to sit outside on the balcony. After talking for some time, Ellen noticed that I was getting cold, so she got up, asked me where she could find a shawl and put it around my shoulders. I noticed Conny's face, just beaming, with eyes that seemed to say, 'See! You prayed for that "someone" who would take care of you and love you and here she is.' It was a testimony for Conny as well, knowing that Ellen would take her place.

On Conny's wedding day, September 1, 1967, the Lord filled the empty place left behind by Conny with Ellen, the tall, fair-haired nurse. Conny and her husband lived not far from us and she took much time to help Ellen with the work. Almost a year after Conny was married, her husband had to go to India for several weeks. During that time, Conny accompanied me to the United States to start the work on the book *The Hiding Place* while Ellen took care of the work in Holland. Yes, it was Conny who started to type that book which has already blessed so many lives all over the world. I knew that she loved the work we were doing but she also missed her husband. It was so good to bring him daily before the Lord. Our prayers were answered and

Conny's husband returned safely to Holland while I continued my travels with my new companion, Ellen.

Two years had passed when we learned that Conny had been taken ill. We returned to Holland and were on our way to visit Conny in the hospital. I knew that she was very ill, because she had received treatment that would indicate terminal illness unless the Lord would perform a miracle. When we entered Conny's room, it was like stepping into a flower garden and in the midst of it was Conny, almost asleep. Her husband was sitting beside her. That day, her specialist had informed her of her illness and that there was no hope. Conny was prepared to go and be with her Lord and Saviour but to take that trip all by herself was so difficult for her. Would Jesus ask that of her?

Slowly she said, 'I have taken many trips in my lifetime but there was always someone with me. Mother was there when I was small, Corrie was with me during many of them, and now my husband is with me. But on this trip, who is going to go with me?'

Her husband gently took her hand and said, 'Conny, here is my hand and as soon as Jesus comes for you, I will surrender your hand to Him!'

Conny did not answer but her face looked content. Suddenly she turned to us and asked us to sing Psalm Twenty-Three for her. I swallowed the lump in my throat and asked the Lord to help me in joining the others in the singing, but the phrase we left out was, 'though I walk through the valley of the shadow of death . . .'

When we finished Conny said, 'You forgot one phrase — please sing it!'

So we sang, 'though I walk through the valley of the shadow of death' while the tears rolled down our cheeks. Then Conny thought of all the friends all over the world whom we had come to know and love, and she asked me to greet them. We began to pray and Conny laid her hands on Ellen's head and said, 'Be . . . faithful unto death and I will give thee a crown of life' (Revelation 2:10).

Conny died a victorious death. Her life bore much fruit, and she prepared many people to meet the Master, our Lord Jesus Christ, who came to call her home to be with Him forever.

And these signs shall follow them that believe;
In my name shall they cast out devils. . . .

Mark 16:17

10 Authority Over Demons

For weeks I had been travelling through Eastern Europe: Russia, Poland, Czechoslovakia — speaking in many home groups and even, on occasion, in a church. Many churches were still open in Eastern Europe, although the Communists were very strict about who could speak — and what they said. However, as a harmless old Dutch woman I was allowed to sometimes speak in one of the churches.

As if by a miracle, I was invited to speak in a series of meetings in a great cathedral in a large Communist city. I found that the pastors loved the Lord and had a heavy burden for lost souls.

The first several nights I spoke about the abundant life in Jesus Christ — the joy, the unspeakable love, and the peace that passes all understanding. It was as though I was carried by the Holy Spirit through the joyful storehouse of abundance that we possess when we know Jesus. I described in great detail the precious promises made available to us in Christ.

But something was wrong. Although some of the people rejoiced, most of them simply sat rooted to their benches. They were like chained animals, dying of hunger but unable to reach the food. And the more I tried to give them the more I was aware their hearts were shackled so they could not taste the food I was offering them.

Each night I would return to my room with a heavy heart for I knew that although these dear people wanted to receive what I was giving them, they could not. 'It is as if the devil keeps a fence around these people that you cannot reach them,' my travelling companion said.

'Could it be that demons keep them in bondage?' I wondered.

I opened my Bible and read, 'In my name shall they cast out devils.'

'Lord, what must I do?' I cried out.

'Obey Me!' came the answer.

'But how, Lord? There are so many who are bound by demon powers and I cannot meet with each of them individually.'

'Where did I say that you can deal only with individuals?' He asked.

I was confused and returned to His Word. It became apparent that the Lord wanted me to send all the evil spirits away in His Name. Yet I knew this type of ministry was forbidden in Communist lands.

That night was the final night of the meetings. The great cathedral was crowded with people, but it was the same as on all the other nights. They were not able to receive what I was giving them. I spoke again on Jesus the Victor. 'In the world you will have tribulation, but be of good courage, I have overcome the world.' (*See* John 16:33.) They sat like stone images, unable to grasp the joy of the Lord.

I knew God was calling on me to act. I trembled, but I had no choice. 'I must interrupt my message for a moment, friends,' I said. 'Many of you cannot grasp the richness the Lord offers us this evening. The servants of Satan are keeping you in bondage.'

Then I obeyed. Taking a deep breath and offering one last quick prayer I said in a loud voice, 'In the Name of Jesus I command all dark powers keeping people from the blessings of God to disappear. Go away! Get out of the hearts of these people. Get out of this church. Go to the place where God sends you.'

Then, closing my eyes I raised my hands upward and prayed, 'Lord, will You now protect us with Your precious blood. *Amen.*'

I was afraid but I felt secure. I knew God had told me to do it. Then, as I opened my eyes and looked out over the huge congregation, I saw a miracle happen. The people who had been in bondage came alive. They began to rejoice and as I continued my message I could sense their eager hearts drinking in the living water as I poured it out before them.

After the service I was scheduled to meet with a large group of local pastors who had attended the meeting. By the time I was able to break away from the crowd of people who came forward to speak to me, and get to the back room, the pastors were already meeting. Their conversation was very serious.

'How could you do that?' one pastor asked as soon as I entered the room. 'Communists do not allow people to speak about demons!'

'I had to obey God,' was my only answer.

The pastors resumed their discussion about the meeting. They, too, had seen the bondage. They had also sensed the release when the demons were cast out. But there were some who had studied psychology and others who had studied demonology. They entered into a heated argument about the subject. I had studied none of these. All I knew was God had told me to use my authority in the Name of Jesus. So I sat back while the argument swirled around me.

At last one of the pastors said, 'We know God's promises

and God's command, but who among us has ever been willing to obey Mark 16:17: "And these signs shall follow them that believe; In my name shall they cast out devils..."'

There was a long, uncomfortable silence. When the Bible interferes with man's theology, it always causes a strain. The pastor then continued, 'God has this evening given Corrie the grace to take the authority of Jesus and in His Name cast out devils. We should be thankful instead of all this arguing.'

That was the end of the pastors' meeting, but, oh, what a lesson I learned that night. It is tragic to be around people, especially men of God, who do not recognize the fact that we are surrounded, not only by angels, but also by the powers of darkness.

Someone once asked my opinion of the missionaries in a certain country. My answer was, 'They have given all, but they have not taken all. They have given homeland, time, money, luxury, and more; but they have not taken all of the boundless resources of God's promises. Many do not know about two precious weapons: the power of the blood of Jesus — and every Christian's legal right to use the wonderful Name of Jesus to cast out demons.'

In *War on the Saints*, Mrs. Jessie Penn-Lewis wrote, '... when the existence of evil spirits is recognized by the heathen, it is generally looked upon by the missionary as "superstition" and ignorance; whereas the ignorance is often on the part of the missionary, who is blinded by the prince of the power of the air to the revelation given in the Scriptures, concerning the satanic powers.'

We need to recognize the enemy in order to overcome him. But let us beware of the mistakes that C. S. Lewis described in *Screwtape Letters*. He says, 'There are two equal and opposite errors into which our race can fall about the devils. One is to disbelieve in their existence, the other is to believe and to feel an unhealthy interest in them! They themselves are equally pleased by both errors, and they hail a materialist or a magician with the same delight.'

We have a good safeguard and guide — the Bible — God's Word. Here we find not only the necessary information about Satan and demons, but also the weapons and the armour that we need for this battle.

God wants and expects us to be conquerors over the powers of darkness — not only for the sake of personal victory and the liberation of other souls — but for His glory, so that His triumph and victory over His enemies may be demonstrated!

First, then, let us see what the Bible says about the powers of darkness. The devil (or Satan) is introduced to us as a person who opposes God and His work. He is the 'god of this world' who blinds the minds of the people to the truths of God's Word. Having rebelled against God, he was cast out of heaven; then, he caused man's fall in paradise. Jesus calls him 'the father of lies, a liar, a murderer.' (*See* John 8:44.) He works often as an 'angel of light', seeking the ruin of the elect. But he was cursed of God. Jesus triumphed over him at the Cross of Calvary and in His Resurrection. He has been condemned and will finally be destroyed.

There are many kinds of demons, and they afflict people in various ways. They also bring false doctrine, trying to seduce the elect by oppressing, obsessing, and possessing. They know Jesus, recognize His power, and tremble before Him. For them, hell is the final destination, as it is for Satan.

Second, the Bible gives us direction concerning the stand we have to take against these powers. It is most important to realize that ours is the position *in Christ*. We are called to resist the devil in the 'whole armour of God', by virtue of the blood of Jesus, by faith, prayer, and fasting.

73

I remember in Ravensbruck, for instance, when we had very little to eat, my sister Betsie said, 'Let us dedicate this involuntary fast to the Lord that it may become a blessing.' Almost immediately we found we had power over the demons that were tormenting us and were able to exercise that power to cast them out of our barracks.

Let us remember that God's Word stands forever, and that His commandments mean for us today exactly the same as for His disciples twenty centuries ago. Those who act on them, in obedience, will in the same way prove God's almighty power. Yes, Jesus said, 'In my name shall they cast out devils.' And that means us today.

Our fight is not against a physical army, a political party, an atheistic organization — or anything like that. Our fight is against organizations and powers that are spiritual. Demons may come in as a result of occult sin, even from years back. This includes contact with hypnotism, astrology charts, fortune-telling, Ouija boards and other forms of occultism, sometimes entered into 'just for fun'. These demons will remain until they are cast out in Jesus' Name.

We are up against the unseen power that controls this dark world and the spiritual agents are from the very headquarters of evil. Therefore, we must wear the 'whole armour of God', that we may be able to resist evil in its day of power, and that even when we have fought to a standstill, we may still stand our ground.

Conny and I had travelled throughout Poland. Conny was then my constant companion, and we met many wonderful Christians in that Iron Curtain country. It encouraged us to know that God was using us to bring comfort and strength to the men and women of God. However, the longer we stayed in Poland, the more exhausted we became.

'I do not understand it,' Conny said one morning as we

were getting up. 'I have just wakened from a full night's sleep but already I am weak and tired.'

I, too, felt the same way. We thought perhaps it was some kind of sickness we had picked up; yet neither of us seemed to be really sick.

Then in Warsaw one day we happened to meet an old friend from Holland. Kees was in Poland with his wife, travelling with his camping trailer.

'What a joy to meet you,' he said. 'How are things going?'

I looked at Conny and she looked at me. 'You know, Kees, we both feel so tired. It is as if our legs are heavy, like when you have the flu. Yet we are not ill, just tired.'

Kees looked at us intently. 'Is this your first time to work in Poland?'

'Yes,' I answered. 'But what does that have to do with it?'

'Let me explain,' Kees said. 'Your tiredness is nothing less than an attack of the devil. He does not like your work in Poland, for the antichrist is busy here, arranging his army.'

Reaching out, he put his hand on my arm. 'Corrie and Conny, you must remember you have the protection of the blood of Jesus. Whenever you experience these attacks from the dark powers, you must rebuke them in the Name of Jesus.'

I knew what Kees was saying was right. We sat in his car while he read from the Bible. 'They overcame him by the blood of the lamb, and by the word of their testimony, and they loved not their lives unto the death' (Revelation 12:11).

Then Kees prayed with us, laying his hands on us in the Name of Jesus and rebuking the dark powers that would attack us. Even as he was praying I felt the darkness leave.

By the time the prayer was over, we both felt covered by the blood of the Lamb and all our tiredness had disappeared.

God had taught us a valuable lesson that we would remember in many other areas of the world. We learned that in a country where a godless philosophy reigns, that only by claiming the blood of Jesus can you stand and not fall. The same is true in a city, or school, or even a church building. If Jesus Christ is not recognized as Supreme, then darkness rules.

Since then we have travelled in many countries and felt this same tiredness coming over us. Often I have felt it in American cities. Now I know it simply means that I am in a place where Satan rules. But praise the Lord! I can be an overcomer when I stand in the power of the blood of the Lamb.

But I say unto you, Love your enemies, bless them that curse you, do good to them that hate you, and pray for them which despitefully use you, and persecute you.

Matthew 5:44

11 Lights From Darkest Africa

Thomas was a tall black man who lived in a round hut together with his big family in the middle of Africa. He loved the Lord and loved people — an unbeatable combination.

Thomas's neighbour, who lived across the dirt street, hated God – and hated men like Thomas who loved God. The hatred grew stronger and stronger until the man began sneaking over at night and setting fire to the straw roof on Thomas's hut, endangering his small children. Three nights in a row this happened and each time Thomas was able to rush out of his hut and put out the flames before they destroyed the roof and the walls. The fact that he never said an unkind word to his neighbour, only showing him love and forgiveness, made his neighbour hate him even more.

One night the neighbour sneaked across the street and set fire to Thomas's roof. This night, however, a strong wind came up and as Thomas rushed to beat out the fire, the sparks blew across the street and set the neighbour's house on fire. Thomas finished putting out the fire on his roof and then rushed across the street to put out the fire on his neighbour's roof. He was able to extinguish the flames, but in the process he badly burned his hands and arms.

Other neighbours told the chief of the tribe what had happened. The chief was so furious that he sent his police to arrest the neighbour and throw him into prison.

That night Thomas came to the meeting where I was speaking (as he had done each night). I noticed his badly burned hands and asked him what had happened. Reluctantly he told me the story.

'It is good that this man is now in prison,' I said. 'Now your children are no longer in danger and he cannot try again to put your house in flames.'

'That is true,' he said. 'But I am so sorry for that man. He is an unusually gifted man and now he must live together with all those criminals in a horrible prison.'

'Then let us pray for him,' I said.

Thomas dropped to his knees and holding up his burned and bandaged hands, he began to pray. 'Lord, I claim this neighbour of mine for You. Lord, give him his freedom and do the miracle that in the future he and I will become a team to bring the Gospel in our tribe. *Amen.*'

Never had I heard such a prayer.

Two days later I was able to go to the prison. I spoke to the prisoners about God's joy and God's love. Among the group who listened intently was Thomas's neighbour. When I asked who would receive Jesus in his heart, that man was the first one to raise his hand.

After the meeting I told him how Thomas loved him, how he had burned his hands trying to put out the fire to save his house, and how he had prayed that they might become a team to spread the Gospel. The man wept big tears and nodded his head saying, 'Yes, yes, that is how it shall be.'

The next day I told Thomas. He praised God and said, 'You see, God has worked a miracle. We never can expect too much from Him.' He left, running off down the path, his face beaming with joy.

I had been in Africa for three weeks when I finally got to visit the prison on the outside of the city. I inquired of the warden if I could talk to the prisoners.

'Impossible,' he said, 'the prison is on restriction for an entire month due to an uprising that has broken out among the prisoners. Nobody is allowed in to see the men, much less give a sermon.'

I felt discouraged but knew that God had brought me to that place for some reason. So, I just stood — looking at the warden.

He grew very uncomfortable (having me stand and look at him). At last he said, 'There are some political prisoners who have been sentenced to death. Would you like to speak to them?'

'Certainly,' I said.

The warden called three heavily armed soldiers who escorted me down a long hall past many barred doors and into a cell where one man was sitting on a low bench which was also his bed. There was absolutely nothing else in the cell. The only light came from a small window high above the floor that let just a little spot of sunlight fall on the hard-packed dirt floor in that dreary place.

I leaned against the wall. He was a young man with black skin and very white teeth. He looked up, his eyes filled with sadness. What could I say? 'Lord, give me some light to pass on to this man who sits in such darkness.'

Finally I asked him a question. 'Do you know about Jesus?'

'Yes,' he said slowly, 'I have a Bible at home. I know that Jesus died on a cross for the sins of the world. Many years ago I accepted Him as my Saviour and followed Him for some time until political affairs absorbed all my time. Now I wish I could start again and live a surrendered life, but it is too late. This week I die.'

'It is not too late, my friend,' I said. 'Do you know the ones responsible for your death sentence?'

'I could give you the entire list of those who have put me here,' he answered, gritting his teeth. 'I know all their names and hate them.'

I opened my Bible and read, 'But if you do not forgive men their trespasses, neither will your Father forgive your trespasses.' Then I closed the Bible and looked at him. 'Do you want your Father to forgive you before you die?'

'Of course I want that,' he said. 'More than anything else in the world. But I cannot meet the conditions. I am not able to forgive. I am young, strong, and healthy. I have a wife and children. These men have wronged me and now this very week they will take away my life. How do I forgive that?'

The man looked at me with eyes full of despair and hopelessness. I felt such a great compassion in my heart, yet I knew I must be stern for much depended on it.

'Let me tell you a story,' I said. And then I told him of my experience in the church in Berlin when my former guard from the concentration camp asked me to forgive him.

'That moment I felt a great bitterness swelling in my heart,' I said. 'I remembered the sufferings of my dying sister. But I knew that unforgiveness would do more harm to me than the guard's whip. So I cried out to the Lord, "Lord, thank You for Romans 5:5:

The love of God is shed abroad in our hearts by the Holy Ghost which is given unto us.

Thank You, Lord, that Your love in me can do that which I cannot do."

'At that moment a great stream of love poured through me and I said, "Brother, give me your hand. I forgive all." '

I looked down at the African man sitting on the bench. 'I could not do it. I was not able. Jesus in me was able to do it. You see, you never touch so much the ocean of God's love as when you love your enemies.'

The man listened as I told him more of Jesus. Then, promising to meet him on the other shore, I prayed with him and left.

The next day a missionary friend came by the place where I was staying. He told me that as soon as I left the prison the prisoner had sent a message to his wife saying, 'Don't hate the people who brought me here and who will cause my death. Love them. Forgive them. I cannot, and neither can you, but Jesus in us can do it.'

I slept well that night, knowing why God had brought me to Africa.

I had spoken in many prisons in my travels across the world, but the prison in Ruanda, Africa, was the dreariest, darkest prison I had ever seen. The men were all black, their uniforms were black and they were sitting in the mud on the ground.

I had just entered the prison gate with my interpreter, a missionary lady. Steam (the aftermath of a hard tropical rain) was rising from the mud. The men were sitting on pieces of paper, branches, banana leaves, their legs caked with mud up to their knees.

'Why don't we go into the building?' I asked my interpreter.

'Impossible,' she whispered, obviously afraid of the men, 'There are so many prisoners that even during the night only half of them can go inside.'

I looked at their faces. Like their skin, their eyes were

dark. It was the look I had seen so many times in Ravensbruck — the look of those whose hope had died. Unhappiness. Despair. Hopelessness. Anger. How could I speak to them? What could I, an old Dutch woman, say to these miserable men that would help their lives?

'Lord,' I prayed, 'I am not able to overcome this darkness.'

'Take My promise of Galatians 5:22,' I heard an inner voice say.

Quickly I took my Bible and opened it to that passage. 'But the fruit of the Spirit is love . . .'

'Thank You, Lord,' I whispered. 'But I have a great love for these men already or I would not be here.'

I read on. 'But the fruit of the Spirit is love, joy . . .'

'Joy?' I asked. 'In these surroundings?' Then I remembered what Nehemiah said, 'The joy of the Lord is my strength.'

'Yes, Lord,' I cried out. 'That is what I need. That is what I claim. I claim the promise of joy.'

Even as I spoke the words I felt a wonderful, lifting sensation in my heart. It was joy — more joy than I had ever felt. It poured like a river out of my inner being; like the rising tide it covered the salt flats of my depression and turned the ugly mud of despair into a shimmering lagoon of blessedness. Moments later I was introduced to the prisoners who all sat, staring at me in hatred. The steam rose around them and the stinging insects swarmed their mud-coated ankles and legs.

I began to talk of the joy that is ours when we know Jesus. What a Friend we have in Him. He is always with us. When we are depressed, He gives us joy. When we do wrong, He gives us the strength to be good. When we hate, He fills us with His forgiveness. When we are afraid, He causes us to love.

82

Several faces changed and I saw that some of my joy was spilling over on them. But I knew what the rest were thinking. *After your talk you can go home, away from this muddy, stinking prison. It is easy to talk about joy when you are free. But we must stay here.*

Then I told them a story.

'Morning roll call at Ravensbruck was often the hardest time of the day. By 4:30 A.M. we had to be standing outside our barracks in the black pre-dawn chill, in blocks of one hundred women, ten wide, ten deep.

'Names were never used in the concentration camp. It was part of the plan to dehumanize the prisoners — to take away their dignity of life — their worth before God and man. I was known simply as Prisoner 66730.

'Roll call sometimes lasted three hours and every day the sun rose a little later and the icy-cold wind blew a little stronger. Standing in the grey of the dawn I would try to repeat, through shivering lips, that verse of Scripture which had come to mean so much to me: 'Who shall separate us from the love of Christ? shall tribulation, or distress, or persecution, or famine, or nakedness, or peril, or sword? As it is written, for thy sake we are killed all the day long; we are accounted as sheep for the slaughter" (Romans 8:35, 36). In all this there was an overwhelming victory through Jesus who had proved His love for me by dying on the cross.

'But there came a time when repeating the words did not help. I needed more. "Oh God," I prayed, "reveal Yourself somehow."

'Then one morning the woman directly in front of me sank to the ground. In a moment a young woman guard was standing over her, a whip in her hand.

' "Get up," she screamed in a rage. "How dare you think you can lie down when everyone else is standing!"

83

'I could hardly bear to see what was happening in front of me. *Surely this is the end of us all*, I thought. Then suddenly a skylark started to sing high in the sky. The sweet, pure notes of the bird rose on the still cold air. Every head turned upward, away from the carnage before us, listening to the song of the skylark soaring over the crematorium. The words of the psalmist ran through my mind: "For as the heaven is high above the earth, so great is [God's] mercy towards them that fear Him (Psalms 103:11)." '

I looked out at the men who were sitting in front of me. No longer were their faces filled with darkness and anger. They were listening — intently — for they were hearing from someone who had walked where they were now walking. I continued.

'There in that prison I saw things from God's point of view. The reality of God's love was just as sure as the cruelty of men.

O love of God, how deep and great,
Far deeper than man's deepest hate.

'Every morning for the next three weeks, just at the time of roll call, the skylark appeared. In his sweet song I heard the call of God to turn my eyes away from the cruelty of men to the ocean of God's love.

'A Jewish doctor, Viktor Frankl, who went through far more suffering in the concentration camps than I, wrote a book. He ends the book with these words: ". . . we have come to know man is that being who has invented the gas chambers of Auschwitz; however, he is also that being who has entered those gas chambers upright with the Lord's Prayer or the *Shema Yisroel* on his lips." '

Although I was speaking through an interpreter, God's Spirit was working through both of us. I saw joy appearing on the faces of nearly all the men sitting before me.

'Say, men,' I said, 'do you know Jesus is willing to live in your hearts? He says, "I stand at the door of your heart and knock. If anyone hears my voice and opens the door, I come in." Just think: that same Jesus loves you and will live in your heart and give you joy in the midst of all this mud. He who is willing, raise his hand.'

I looked around. All the men, including the guards, had raised their hands. It was unbelievable, but their faces showed a joy that only the Holy Spirit could produce. As I left the prison and returned to the car, all the men accompanied me. The guards did not seem worried or anxious that they swarmed around me. In fact, they did not even prevent them from going out the gate to stand around my car. As I opened the door and got in, the men began to shout and chant something, repeating the same words over and over.

'What do they shout?' I asked my interpreter. She smiled and said, 'They shout, "Old woman, come back. Old woman, come back and tell us more of Jesus." '

The missionary turned to me as we drove off. 'I must confess to you that I thought this place was too dark for the light of the Gospel. I had been here once before and was so frightened I said I would never come back. Now, because I had to come to interpret for you, I have seen what the Holy Spirit can do. The joy of the Lord is available, even for such a place as this. From now on I shall return every week to tell them about Jesus.'

Months later I received a letter from her in which she said, 'The fear is gone. The joy remains.'

*Carry neither purse, nor scrip, nor shoes: and
salute no man by the way . . . And in the
same house remain, eating and drinking such
things as they give: for the labourer is worthy
of his hire. . . .*

Luke 10:4, 7

12   God Will Provide

The people in America seem to feel I should not hesitate to
ask for money for my ministry, which supports other
ministries such as Bible and book translations in many parts
of the world. However, from the very beginning of my
ministry I have felt it was wrong to ask for money – even
to ask for travel expenses. I did not want to be paid for
'services rendered'. I simply wanted to preach the Gospel
and let the Lord provide for me.

I learned this lesson very early in my travelling ministry. I
was in New England and spoke, among other things, about
the former concentration camp where I helped refugees in
Germany. My hosts had asked me to do this, saying they
knew the American people would like to help support it.
After the meeting a dignified, well-dressed lady came up and
handed me a cheque for a rather large sum of money. It
was designated to my work in Europe.

'It was so very interesting to hear about your work,' she
said.

'What did you think about the other things I said?' I
asked. 'Did you find them important also?'

She gave me a quizzical look. I continued. 'Of course it is
a very good thing to give money for evangelistic work, but

today I also spoke about conversion. God does not want a little bit of your money, He wants all of your heart. He wants to possess you completely. God will not let me take your cheque.' I handed it back to her.

As I was speaking I noticed a haughty, proud look come into her eyes. Very deliberately she pulled her fur cape around her neck. Then, without answering at all, she arrogantly walked away.

When I got back to my room I looked sadly at the other cheques which had been given me. Was God speaking to me? Was it wrong to speak of my own work while at the same time I urged people to be converted or to forgive their enemies? Was it wrong to listen to these Americans who were urging me to receive collections for my ministry? I dropped to my knees in prayer. God knew my needs.

The answer was very clear from the Lord. 'From now on you must never again ask for money.'

Great joy entered my heart and I prayed, 'Heavenly Father, You know that I need more money than ever before. But from this day on I shall never ask for a penny. No guarantees before I come to speak. No travel expenses. Not even a place to stay. I will trust in You believing that You will never forsake me.'

That very day I received two letters. One was from a woman in Switzerland. 'Corrie, God told me that from now on you must never again ask for money.'

The other letter was from my sister in Holland. She wrote, 'When I prayed for your work this morning God made it clear to me that you should not ask anybody for financial support. He will provide everything.'

I thought of the night in the concentration camp when my sister Betsie had talked with me about our plans for the future. 'Corrie, we should never worry about money,' she said. 'God is willing to supply our every need.'

87

Many years later, when I faced a severe hardship, I was forced to remember this principle. I felt I had received a direct command from the Lord to go to Russia. The price of our tickets and expenses would be five thousand guilders. However, when I looked at my cheque book I found we had only three thousand guilders in the bank.

'Lord,' I prayed, 'what must I do? You have commanded me to go to Russia but I need two thousand more guilders.'

I thought that this time God would let me write a few wealthy friends, telling them of my need, and asking them to send the money for the plane ticket. Instead I heard a very clear directive from God: 'Give away two thousand guilders.'

'Oh, no, Lord,' I said, as I sat at the table in my apartment in Baarn, Holland. 'You did not understand. I did not say I wanted to *give* away two thousand guilders. I said I needed someone to give me that amount so I could go to Russia.'

However, God seldom listens to my arguments. He waited for me to get through with my objections, and then repeated His original command. This time, though, it was even more specific. I was to give two thousand guilders to a certain mission group that had an immediate need.

I could not understand how anyone's need could be more immediate than my own, but foregoing the 'wisdom of the wise', I sat down and wrote a cheque to this mission group, depleting my bank account down to one thousand guilders.

Later that day I went back down to see if I had received any mail. Among the letters was one from the American publishing company that was to publish *The Hiding Place*. For some months I had been writing back and forth and only two weeks before I had finally signed the contract. I brought the letter back upstairs and opened it. As I pulled it out, a cheque fluttered to the floor. It was an advance from the publisher, money which I did not think I was going to get until the manuscript was completed. I looked at the figure. It amounted to more than I needed!

God takes His prohibition of asking for money very seriously, just as He means it seriously when He says He will care for and protect us. However, if we seek to raise our own money then God will let us do it — by ourselves. Many times we will be able to raise great amounts of money by human persuasion or downright perseverance in asking. But we will miss the far greater blessing of letting Him supply all our needs according to His own riches. And, as I found out in the case of the guilders needed for the trip to Russia, God always has more for us than we would think of asking.

I would much rather be the trusting child of a rich Father, than a beggar at the door of worldly men.

Yes, the Lord is not only my shepherd; He is my treasurer. He is very wealthy. Sometimes He tries my faith, but when I am obedient then the money always comes in just in time.

My last stop on my first trip to the Orient was Formosa. It was time for me to move on so I went to the travel agency in Taipei and gave the girl a list of all the places I needed to go on the next leg of my journey. Hong Kong, Sydney, Auckland, then back to Sydney, on to Cape Town, Tel Aviv and finally to Amsterdam.

The travel agent wrote it all down and then asked, 'What is your final destination?'

'Heaven,' I answered simply.

She gave me a puzzled look. 'How do you spell that?

'H-E-A-V-E-N,' I spelled out slowly.

After she had written it down she sat looking at the paper. At last she looked up. 'Oh, now I understand,' she said with a smile. 'But I did not mean that.'

'But I meant it,' I said. 'And you do not need to write it down because I already have my ticket.'

'You have a ticket to *heaven*?' she asked, astonished. 'How did you receive it?'

'About two thousand years ago,' I said, noting her genuine interest, 'there was One who bought my ticket for me. I only had to accept it from Him. His name is Jesus and He paid my fare when He died on the cross for my sins.'

A Chinese clerk, working at the next desk, overheard our conversation and joined in. 'What the old woman says is true,' he told his companion.

I turned and looked at the Chinese man. 'Have you a reservation for heaven?' I asked him.

His face lit up in a smile. 'Yes, I have,' he said, nodding enthusiastically. 'Many years ago, as a child on the mainland, I received Jesus as my Saviour. That makes me a child of God with a place reserved in the house of the Father.'

'Then you are also my brother,' I said, shaking his hand. Turning back to the other clerk I said, 'When you do not have a reservation for a seat on the plane, and try to get aboard, you face difficulty. But when you do not have a place reserved for you in heaven, and the time comes for you to go, you end up in far greater difficulty. I hope my young brother here will not rest until you have made your reservation in heaven.'

The Chinese clerk smiled broadly, and nodded. I felt confident he would continue to witness to his fellow worker now that I had opened the door.

I left the travel agency with a good feeling in my heart. Surely God was going to bless this trip since I was already off to such a good start. However, when I arrived in my room and checked my ticket, I found the girl had made a mistake in the route. Instead of sending me from Sydney to Cape Town to Tel Aviv, as I had requested, she had routed

90

me from Sydney to Tel Aviv and then to Cape Town. I went immediately to the phone and called her.

'Why have you changed my schedule?' I asked. 'My Chief has told me I must go first to Cape Town and after that to Tel Aviv. However, you have changed the sequence. God is my Master and I must obey Him.'

'Then God has made a mistake,' she said, half-seriously. 'There is no direct flight from Australia to Africa since there is no island in the Indian Ocean for the plane to land and refuel. That is why you must first go overland to Tel Aviv and then down to Cape Town.'

'No,' I argued. 'I cannot follow that route. I must do what my Chief has told me. I'll just have to pray for an island in the Indian Ocean.'

We both laughed and hung up. 'Lord,' I prayed, 'if I have made a mistake in hearing Your direction, please show me. But if I heard correctly, then open the way.'

An hour later the girl called back. 'Did you really pray for an island in the Indian Ocean?' she asked, incredulous. Before I could answer she continued, 'I just received a telegram from Qantas, the Australian airline. They have just begun to use the Cocos Islands for a refueling station and beginning tomorrow will have a direct flight from Sydney to Cape Town.'

I thanked her and hung up. It was good to know that God does not make a mistake in His plans.

However, I am stubborn and never seem to learn my lessons well. Just a few days later, after I got to Sydney and was to make a short trip to Auckland, New Zealand, and back, I ran into another situation which would have been much easier on me had I remembered the lesson I should have learned back in Formosa.

Since I was only going to be in Auckland for four days before returning to Sydney and then on to Cape Town, I packed all my essential items into one suitcase which I would carry with me. I left the other suitcases with my friends in Sydney, planning to pick them up when I came back through on my way to Africa. Besides my essential clothing, I also took with me my notebooks, Bibles, literature, and coloured slides. My slides, taken in many lands, and the manuscripts of my sermons are all very valuable to me. Although I seldom read from my notes when I speak, I feel more comfortable when I have them before me. I have been accused by my friends of ascending the platform with three Bibles and five notebooks. I think it is hardly that bad, but I have met so many people and jotted down so many ideas that I cannot remember them all. So I try to carry all my notes with me.

As I started to leave the Sydney airport for the plane, one of the pilots spotted me struggling along with my heavy suitcase. He volunteered to help me. 'I have to stop by the radio room first,' he said, 'but then I shall bring your bag directly to your seat.'

I hesitated to turn loose my bag, however, since it was filled with everything I needed for the rest of my journey, not to mention a lifetime of treasures.

'You can trust me,' he insisted. 'I will arrive at the plane before you and shall leave your bag on your seat.'

Reluctantly I parted from my suitcase and watched the pilot as he walked out of the door. Several minutes later we boarded the plane and I rushed to my seat. The bag was not there. Alarmed, I called the stewardess. She assured me that the bag had been stowed with the rest of the luggage and was perfectly safe. I tried to settle back in my seat as we took off, yet I had an uncomfortable feeling inside.

The plane made a stop in Melbourne before heading out over the Tasman Sea for New Zealand. However, when we landed in Melbourne there was a radio message waiting for me. Like Job, the thing which I greatly feared had come upon me. The message was from Sydney. A bag, belonging to Corrie ten Boom, had been left in the radio room.

I was frustrated — and angry. 'Can they send it to me?' I asked the ticket agent.

'I'm sorry,' he said, shaking his head. 'The only way we can get it to you is to send it on our next plane to London. From there it will go to Rome, then Tel Aviv, and then . . .'

'Oohhh,' I groaned, waving him quiet. 'It will never make it. It contains all my earthly treasures and it is not even locked. Tell them just to hold it for me in Sydney. I shall pick it up when I return in four days. In the meantime, I have nothing, not even a toothbrush.'

I reboarded the plane and slumped in my seat, dejected, angry, and full of resentment. On the flight from Sydney to Melbourne I had witnessed to the stewardess about my faith in Jesus Christ. I had told her that Jesus was victor in every situation and that He gave us the power to praise Him in all situations. Now, however, I did not feel very much like praising Him at all.

I looked up and the stewardess was bending over me. 'How wonderful it must be to be a Christian at a time like this,' she said. 'Most people would be full of anger and resentment.'

I forced a smile and said, 'Well, it must be for some reason; nothing happens by chance to a child of God.'

Even though I was speaking the truth, I was not walking in the victory. Victory would mean that I had no resentment at all, and at that moment I was overflowing with it.

It was late evening as the plane took off from Melbourne. It would be a night flight to Auckland and I tried to make myself comfortable. Below us was the sea with only the engines of the plane to hold us in the sky. I dozed, fitfully, and then woke to the smell of smoke in the cabin. The other passengers were awake also, and some of them were up in the aisle, expressing alarm. Moments later the stewardess was at my seat.

'I have good news for you,' she said softly. 'We are returning to Sydney to pick up your bag.'

'Yes, indeed, good news for me,' I said. 'But tell me, are we not in great danger?'

'No,' she said, smiling sweetly and patting my pillow, 'we are just having some hydraulic difficulties. There is no danger.'

I followed her with my eyes as she went from seat to seat, assuring all the passengers that there was no danger. I leaned across the aisle and asked the man in the next seat what was meant by hydraulic difficulties.

'It is bad news,' he said. 'All the mechanism on the plane depends on the hydraulic system. The wing flaps, the steering mechanism, even the landing gear is controlled by the hydraulic system. Since the fire is in that system it means the pilot could lose control of the plane at any moment.'

I sat back in my seat and tried to look out the window. Below was the blackness of the Tasman Sea. The smell of smoke was still very strong in the cabin. I was not afraid of death. Often, as a prisoner I had faced it. I remembered the words of Dwight Moody, 'The valley of the shadow of death holds no darkness for the child of God. There must be light, else there could be no shadow. Jesus is the Light. He has overcome death.'

Yet I knew I was not right with God because I was not right with man. I still held resentment in my heart and knew it had to be removed before I could even pray. I leaned back in my seat and opened my heart to God, confessing my resentment over my suitcase (which was worthless to me now that we might crash into the sea) and asking Him to forgive me. Then I prayed, 'Lord, perhaps I shall see You very soon. I thank You that all my sins have been cleansed by the blood of the Lamb.'

I opened my eyes and looked around me. 'What of the others?' I wondered. 'Are they prepared to die?' No one was sleeping. All were sitting, alert in their seats. I noticed a woman busy applying lipstick and shook my head. How silly to feel you have to enter eternity with painted lips! I had the strongest urge to stand up and say to the people around me, 'Friends, perhaps in a few minutes we shall all enter eternity. Do you know where you are going? Are you prepared to appear before God? There is still time to accept the Lord Jesus . . .'

But I could say nothing. I wanted to stand and urge them to come to Jesus, but I could not. I was ashamed of the Gospel of our Lord Jesus Christ. And not only that, but there was fear in my heart.

We finally made a landing — safe landing — in Sydney. My bag was returned to me, but there was no joy in my heart. Even though I had been forgiven of my resentment, I had been ashamed of the Lord Jesus. I found a seat in the lounge and sat with my head bowed, my eyes closed.

'Dear Lord, I am not fit to be a missionary. I stood before the very portals of eternity and warned no one.'

I opened one of my notebooks and read on the margin of a page a note I had made many years before. 'To travel through the desert with others, to suffer thirst, to find a spring, to drink of it, and not tell the others that they may be spared is exactly the same as enjoying Christ and not telling others about Him.'

'Oh, Lord,' I moaned. 'Send me back home. Let me repair watches. I am not worthy to be Your evangelist.'

As I sat there, like Jeremiah, trying to resign my commission, I saw a man coming towards me. He introduced himself as a Jewish doctor who had been aboard my flight.

'I watched you all through those hours on the plane when our lives were in great danger,' he said. 'You were neither afraid nor anxious. What is your secret?'

A ray of light. Perhaps God was giving me another chance. 'I am a Christian,' I said joyfully. 'I know the Messiah, Jesus, the Son of God. He died on the cross for my sins, and yours also. If our burning plane had fallen into the sea I had the assurance of going to Heaven.'

We sat and talked for a long time before he excused himself. But a few minutes later he was back again. 'I must hear more about this Jesus who gives you such peace,' he said.

Four times he got up and left, and yet he kept coming back. Each time his request was the same. 'Tell me more about Jesus.'

I told him how Jesus gives us authority over Satan. How Jesus has promised us mansions in heaven. How He gives to all who believe the power to become the sons of God.

The Jewish doctor drank it all in and finally left saying I had given him much to think about. I sat back in my chair. The Lord, my treasurer, had given me just enough of His wealth that I might share it with one of His hungry children. I had been found worthy to evangelize after all. And in the process I had learned another valuable lesson in the school of life. When I am weak, then am I strong (2 Corinthians 12:10).

He shall feed his flock like a shepherd: he shall
gather the lambs with his arm, and carry them
in his bosom. . . .

Isaiah 40:11

13 A Place to Be

Everyone needs a place to be. One of the great joys of
heaven is that it is a place, a prepared place. I am thankful
that there I will have a special house that is reserved just for
me.

When I was born, Father and Mother were living on the
Korte Prinsegracht, a typical Amsterdam canal. I was born
prematurely and my skin was blue. Uncle Hendrik, Tante
Jans's husband, looked at me and exclaimed, 'I hope the
Lord will quickly take this poor little creature to His home
in heaven.'

But my parents and Tante Anna did not agree with him.
They surrounded me with love and care. However, since
there were no incubators in those early days, I cried much
from the cold. Tante Anna, knowing I missed the warmth of
the special place under my mother's heart from which I had
come, rolled me in her apron and tied me against her sto-
mach. There I was warm and quiet.

Many years later I was in a primitive house in Africa. The
bathtub was made from an old oil drum that had been sawed
in half. Missionaries lived there and they invited me in to eat
with them. Walking into the kitchen, I saw an African

woman with the white missionary child strapped tightly to her back.

'Hey, how nice she has your baby on her back,' I said to the missionary mother.

The white mother smiled and said, 'The baby was so fearful this morning. All she would do was cry. When the African cook came to the house she took one look at the baby and said, "Ah, Missee, give me the baby. I will keep her quiet." So she strapped her on her back and the baby has slept all morning while the cook has been busy around the kitchen.'

I could understand that feeling of having a place — of belonging. I was often afraid as a small child. Sleeping beside my sister, Nollie, who was a year and a half older than me, I begged to be able to hold her hand at night. She refused, and instead gave me the hem of her nightgown. By and by she did not even like me holding on to that, but told me to hold on to the hem of my doll's nightgown.

Then, when I was five years old, the Lord Jesus became a great reality to me. My mother told me how He loved little children and was even willing to live in my heart if I asked Him in. I did, and a feeling of peace and security took the place of the fear I had so often felt. From then on I could go to sleep at night and not be afraid.

As a child I prayed a nursery rhyme:

> Ik ga slapen, ik ben moe;
> 'k Sluit mijn oogjes beiden toe.
> Heere, houd ook deze nacht
> Weder over mij de wacht.

> (I'm going to sleep, I am tired;
> I close both my little eyes.
> Lord, watch over me again
> The whole night long.)

In all these years that I have been a 'tramp for the Lord', I have often been afraid. But in those moments I have always reached up and touched the hem of Jesus' garment. He has never failed to wrap me close to Him. Yet, I still long for that time when I shall have a mansion in heaven.

Here on earth, at the age of seventy-seven, for the first time I found a place of my own — a beautiful apartment in Baarn, Holland. Even though I am seldom there (for I intend to keep on travelling until I die in harness), it is still a place to hang up my pictures on the walls and put the few sticks of furniture that I have saved from my days in the Beje. Yet, even with this 'home' here on earth, I still long most of all for my heavenly mansion.

When I was a child, Tante Jans composed a children's song. I remember two lines:

'k zou zoo graag eens komen, Heiland,
In dat heerlijk Vaderhuis.

(I should just like to come, Saviour,
In that beautiful Father-house.)

As a child, however, I always got the words mixed up when I sang the song. Instead of singing, 'to come', I would sing 'to peek'. The older people laughed at my mistake but I thought they were very stupid. With all my heart I meant what I was singing. As a little child I did not want to go to heaven, I just wanted to peek for a moment. Now, though, that my days have grown long, I no longer sing as I did as a child. Now my greatest desire is to come for all eternity into the beautiful Father-house.

Behold, to obey is better than sacrifice . . . .

1 Samuel 15:22

14 Obedience

Obedience is easy when you know you are being guided by a God who never makes mistakes.

Conny and I were in Africa and one day during my Quiet Time I began to feel that God was telling me it was time to leave Africa.

'Lord, where do You want us to go?' I asked.

'Argentina,' came the answer deep in my heart.

Argentina? I had never been to Argentina. I could not speak a word of Spanish. In those days air travel was sometimes poor in Africa and to fly across the Atlantic Ocean to Buenos Aires would be a trying ordeal. Yet as I sat before the Lord the word *Argentina* became even stronger.

'Yes, but . . . ,' I started to answer Him. Then I remembered that obedience never says, 'Yes, but . . .' Rather it always says, 'Yes, Lord!' Some months before a missionary by the name of Breson had written me, asking if I would be willing to speak in his church if I ever came to Argentina. I did not know Breson very well, so I had not thought much about the invitation. Now, however, with God speaking to me so strongly, I sat down and wrote Mr. Breson a letter, asking if he could meet us in Buenos Aires and arrange some meetings for me.

We waited almost a month, but there was no answer. 'Are you sure it is the Lord's guidance for us to go to Argentina?' Conny asked. 'Perhaps this man Breson no longer lives in Buenos Aires. What if we go and there is no one to meet us? Then what will we do?'

I reached out and touched Conny's hand. 'Yes, I know it is God's will for us to go to Argentina. Some years ago God spoke to me and told me to go to Japan. I had no money. I knew no one in Japan. I could not speak the language. Yet I knew God had led me. I finally saved up enough money to fly to Tokyo and stepped off the plane on a dark, rainy night in that strange land and said, "Lord, here I am. Now what?" I remembered that David Morken was there with Youth for Christ. He found me a room and because of my obedience God opened many doors of ministry. I was alone on that trip, but this time I have you. No, I know we should go to Argentina.'

The plane flight was much longer than we expected. Connections were very bad and we had to spend one whole day in a hot, dirty African airport awaiting a connecting flight that would take us on to West Africa for our flight across the ocean. It was almost midnight when we caught our last plane and I could sense Conny's anxiety. However, I was sure of God's guidance.

We finally arrived in the busy Buenos Aires airport. I looked out across the hundreds of hurrying people, hoping I might see Mr. Breson's face. There was no one.

Conny and I struggled with our luggage and at the ticket desk a man asked us, in broken English, if he could send our bags to our address.

'I do not yet know my address,' I said. Conny looked worried. I knew her thoughts. *Do you know for sure it is*

Argentina where God would have you work? We were both exhausted from all-night plane rides which had been added to the ordeal of waiting in all those African airports. We carried our suitcases to the kerb and I sat down. 'See if you can find a taxi,' I said to Conny. 'Perhaps there is a YWCA hotel nearby.'

But there were no taxis. The air was heavy and hot. I finally asked a man, 'Do you know where there is a YWCA hotel?'

The man gave me a blank stare and moved on. I could speak Dutch, German, and English, but none of those languages helped me here. We sat on our suitcases looking at the streams of traffic passing down the street.

'Aunty, Tante Corrie, are you sure that God's guidance brought us to Argentina?'

I looked at Conny. Her face was dirty and creased with lines of exhaustion. I, too, was hot and tired and unhappy. But I was also sure of God's leadership. 'Yes,' I said wearily. 'I am sure.'

'I don't like Argentine mosquitos,' Conny said, slapping her arm. 'They are just as cruel as African mosquitos.'

We looked at each other and laughed. Here we were in a strange country with a strange language. Holland was far, far away, yet we were laughing.

Then I heard a man's voice from the other side of the street shouting, '*Bent u Corrie ten Boom?*' ('Are you Corrie ten Boom?')

My name. My language. What joy! I could barely see the man on the far side of the streaming traffic, but he was waving his arms as he shouted.

'*Ja, dat ben ik,*' I shouted back.

The man had to wait for the traffic to thin before he could run across the street. Finally, after dodging cars, he stepped on to the kerb. 'I am Reverend Mees,' he said, extending his hand. 'I did not think you would be here but felt I should come and check just the same.'

'Do you know Mr. Breson?' I asked. 'I had hoped he would meet us.'

'Did you not receive Breson's letter?' Reverend Mees asked. There was a look of alarm on his face.

'No, we heard nothing from him.'

Reverend Mees put his hand on his forehead and looked towards the sky. 'Oh, this is too bad. He wrote you a letter telling you not to come. He could not arrange any meetings and is now on a mission tour in the jungle. He will not be back for two months.'

I sat back down on my suitcases, feeling even more tired than before.

'Do you know if there is a YWCA hotel in the city?' I asked, as if this would solve all our problems.

Reverend Mees smiled, 'No, I do not know of a YWCA hotel, but a dear friend of mine, a woman doctor, knew about the possibility of your coming. She asked me to bring you to her hospital and from there she will take you to her home. She has a spare bedroom and a little apartment where you can be very comfortable.'

Dr. Gwen Shepherd received us graciously at the hospital. I knew at once that she was one of God's precious children and therefore my sister also. She took us to her car and for the first time I experienced what traffic in Buenos Aires is like. Travelling in the jungles of Africa was nothing to the streets of Buenos Aires. There were no traffic lights. At every intersection the cars came racing together, four abreast. Those who arrived first were the first ones through. I never saw an accident (but perhaps that was because I kept my eyes closed most of the time!). However, after bouncing and speeding down the streets, we finally reached her home where she provided wonderful hospitality. That night she invited a number of youth group leaders to her home and I had an opportunity to share with them. The next day another invitation came for me to speak and before long I was even busier than I had been in any other place on the earth. Dr. Shepherd had a wonderful gift of administration and arranged much ministry for me. It was indeed God's guidance for me to come to Argentina. What a joy I would have missed had I disobeyed.

Perhaps the greatest joy of the entire trip, however, happened one afternoon in Dr. Shepherd's hospital. I was allowed into a ward where polio patients were being treated. One room was filled with people in iron lungs. I had never seen the wheezing, gasping iron lungs before and they scared me.

'Do you wish to talk to some of the patients?' a kind nurse asked me.

I looked around and said, 'No, I think I am unable to talk. I just want to go off somewhere and cry.'

Always when I say that I am not able, I get the same answer from the Lord. He says, 'I know you can't. I have known it already a long time. I am glad now you know it for yourself for now you can let Me do it.'

'All right, Lord, You do it,' I said. And surely the Lord did. I went from one iron lung to another telling the men and women about the Lord Jesus Christ who breathes into each one of us His Holy Spirit.

Then I came to a man on a rocking bed. He had a different kind of polio and instead of being in a lung he was on a bed that rocked up and down. When his head was up he could breathe in. When his head went down he breathed out. The nurse told me he was Jewish.

'Ah,' I said, 'I am happy to meet one of God's chosen people. My old father, my dear sister, and some others in my family died in concentration camps because we loved the

Jews. I, too, was in prison for helping Jews. But tell me, do you know the Jew, Jesus, as your personal Messiah?'

The bed rocked up and down and he shook his head for he could not speak. He had a long tube in his nose and could only move one hand slightly to write tiny notes.

'Then is it all right if I tell you about him?' I asked.

He picked up his stubby pencil and scribbled on a small notebook on the side of his moving bed, 'I am ready to listen.'

I stayed beside that rocking bed and told my Jewish friend about the great Messiah, the one whom the prophet called, 'Wonderful, Counsellor, The mighty God, The everlasting Father, The Prince of Peace' (Isaiah 9:6).

I finished speaking and from my bag took a small embroidery. On one side was stitched a beautiful crown. The other side was quite mixed up. 'When I see you on this bed,' I said, 'not speaking, not moving, I think of this embroidery.' I held up the back side of the embroidery. 'Your life is like this. See how dark it is. See how the threads are knotted and tangled, mixed up. But when you turn it around then you can see that God is actually weaving a crown for your life. God has a plan for your life and He is working it out in beauty.'

He picked up his pencil and wrote again:

*thanks God
I am already
seeing the
beautiful side*

Thanks God I am already seeing the beautiful side.

What a miracle. He understood God did not want him to become a Gentile. Rather he would become a completed Jew. I prayed and thanked the Lord with him. Then it was time to go and Dr. Shepherd once again took me to her beautiful home.

The next day I returned to the polio ward and asked the nurse if I could speak with my Jewish friend.

'I am sorry,' she said, 'but your Jewish friend on the rocking bed is no longer with us. Just five minutes after you left he beckoned me to come to his side. There was a wonderful light shining in his eyes and he wrote on a little paper, "For the first time I prayed in Jesus' name." Then he closed his eyes and died.'

'Then I am not sorry,' I answered. 'I am glad. I know he has his own crown of life. Praise God.'

God has a divine pattern for each of His children. Although the threads may seem knotted — as they did when we were sitting outside the airport in Buenos Aires — on the other side is a crown.

*For my thoughts are not your thoughts, neither
are your ways my ways, saith the Lord.*

Isaiah 55:8

15 The Real Corrie ten Boom

While in Havana, Cuba, I was asked to speak at a youth
rally in the Salvation Army hall. Of course this was before
the Communist take-over so there was still freedom to talk
openly about the Lord Jesus Christ.

It was a hot June night and the hall was small and stifling.
The meeting was scheduled to begin at seven o'clock, but
more and more groups continued to arrive from other parts
of the city, so no one seemed to be in a hurry to start. As in
most Latin American countries everything was, *'Mañana,
mañana'*, even the church services.

Finally, I was seated on the platform between two men
with huge drums. One of them, an old Negro with white
hair, tried to show his love for the Lord by vigorously beating one of the drums. The sound was almost unbearable.
The captain had a very sharp voice and led the singing by
shouting, waving his hands, and pounding on the top of the
pulpit. The young Cubans sang loudly with much clapping
of hands and stomping of feet. By nine o'clock I was already
worn out, and all I had done was sit and listen. There was a
terrific ringing in my ears and my head was splitting with a
headache from the crashing sounds of the drums. Finally,

though, I was called on to speak and the hall grew silent. I was grateful for the few moments of peace.

After I spoke the captain introduced a missionary who had brought his slides. The lights were turned out and we all sat in the miserable heat while the missionary began his long slide presentation. Like many missionaries, he had been called upon to do some medical work in the field, so many of his slides dealt with that. He had photograph after photograph of drugs and medicines which had been given him by various doctors. 'This particular bottle of pills was given me by Dr. Smith,' he droned on. Then flipping to his next slide he said, 'And this box of medicines was sent me by Dr. Jones.'

The young people in the hall were not the least bit interested in seeing these boxes, bottles, and jars. The noise grew louder and louder and finally reached such volume that the missionary had to shout to make himself heard. It was ten-thirty when he finally finished his presentation and the lights came back on.

Now the room was filled with flying bugs, moths, insects, and some kind of huge flying beetle which buzzed around the exposed light bulbs and then dropped to the floor or in people's laps. The young people were climbing over the backs of the benches, babies were asleep on the floor, and everybody was sweating profusely. I did not think I could stand much more.

Then the captain came to the front again and began to preach. A flying insect went in my ear and another was caught in my hair. I looked for some way to escape, but I was boxed in by the huge drums on either side. Finally the captain gave an invitation for people to come forward and be saved.

'Surely no one is in a mood to do anything but go home,' I said to myself. Then I thought, *I hope nobody comes to the front, I long to get out of here and go to bed.*

Yet, to my great surprise, people began getting up from their seats and coming to the front. They were kneeling around the altar rail. Twenty of them. I saw tears in the eyes of some of the young Cubans and listened as the captain spoke with great persuasion, his voice full of love.

A startling realization swept over me. I was selfish. I had hoped nobody would be saved because of my own weariness. My sleep was more important than the salvation of sinners. Oh, what a terrible egotist I was. Suddenly my bed was no longer important. I was willing to stay up all night if God was working. But what could I do with my guilty feeling for having been so selfish?

Then I began to praise God, for I had learned what to do with my sin. I confessed it to the Heavenly Father in Jesus' Name and I claimed His forgiveness. With joy I was able to get up and pray with the twenty young people who had made the important decision to commit their lives to Jesus Christ. It was eleven-thirty when the meeting finally came to a close.

The next morning, Sunday, I spoke in a beautiful church which was filled with the most prominent people in Havana. As I entered the imposing building I was given a copy of the parish magazine which had been handed to all the other people. In it I read an introductory article about my ministry. It said, 'Corrie ten Boom is a most popular world evangelist ... She is tireless and completely selfless in her absolute dedication to the cause of the Gospel . . .'

Oh, Lord, I thought, *if only these people knew who the real Corrie ten Boom is, they would not have come out this morning to hear me.*

'Tell them,' the Lord answered immediately.

By that time I was seated on the platform looking out over the sea of faces before me. 'But Lord, if I tell them, they will reject me.'

'Can I bless a lie?' the Lord asked me in my heart. 'I can only bless the truth. You do want My blessing, don't you?'

Then it was time for me to speak. The gracious minister gave a flowery introduction and asked me to come to the pulpit. Before I could give my message, however, I knew what I had to do.

Reading first from the parish paper I then said, 'Sometimes I get a headache from the heat of the halo that people put around my head. Would you like to know what Corrie ten Boom is really like?' Then I told them what happened the evening before — how my own sleep had been more important in my eyes than the salvation of young people. 'That,' I said, 'was Corrie ten Boom. What egotism! What selfishness! But the joy is that Corrie ten Boom knew what to do with her sins. When I confessed them to the Father, Jesus Christ washed them in His blood. They are now cast into the deepest sea and a sign is put up that says, NO FISHING ALLOWED. Corrie ten Boom is lazy, selfish, and filled with ego. But Jesus in Corrie ten Boom is just the opposite of all these things.'

Then I waited. Surely now that the congregation knew what kind of person I was, they would no longer want to hear me. Instead I sensed them all leaning forward, eager to hear what I might say. Instead of rejecting me, they accepted me. Instead of a beautiful church with prominent members and a popular world evangelist, we were all sinners who knew that Jesus died to lift us out of the vicious circle of ego into the light of His love.

God had blessed the truth!

*For the Son of man is come to seek and to
save that which was lost.*

Luke 19:10

16   Checkpoint Charlie

Conny and I stood in line, along with other people, outside
Checkpoint Charlie, the gate for foreigners into East Berlin.
Many of those in line were Dutch and I saw they were being
passed without difficulty. Everything seemed routine: Hand
your passport to a guard, walk down the line, and receive
your passport back with a stamp that allowed you to spend
the one day in East Berlin. I hoped it would be as easy for us
when it was our turn to be checked.

Finally we were in front of the window. The guard looked
at our passports, looked in a book, and then turned and said
something to another man behind him.

'Is there a problem?' I asked the man.

He turned and gave me a stern look. 'Come with me,' he
said, motioning for Conny and me to follow him into a
small room to one side. We were questioned and then they
opened my handbag. There they found two books. One of
them was one of my books which had been published in East
Germany. The other was a copy of Billy Graham's *Peace
With God* which had also been translated into German.

The officer picked up Billy Graham's book and shouted,
'What? A book by that machine gun of God!'

I laughed. 'I like the name you give to Billy Graham. I will tell him what you called him the next time I see him — God's Machine Gun. However, if I am not allowed to take the books with me into East Berlin, I will just give them to you and you can let us go on.'

'Oh, no,' he said sternly, 'it is not that easy. First we have to write up your deposition.'

He searched me to see if I had hidden more books before he began his inquisition. I did not like his rough, crude manner and told him so.

'I really feel as if I am in the hands of the Gestapo again,' I said.

'No,' he said, abashed, 'I am no Gestapo.'

'You surely have the same manners,' I said bluntly.

He softened his approach but still kept us in the inquisition room for more than three hours. A woman typist copied everything I said and wrote it into a 'protocol'. I learned that my name was on the blacklist for East Germany, which was the reason I was being so thoroughly questioned. However, I was primarily upset because we had only a few hours to visit the Christians in East Berlin and our time was being wasted here in the guard station.

'Lord,' I complained silently, 'why are You keeping us here when we need to be about Your business in East Berlin?'

Then slowly it came through my stubborn Dutch mind that God had us in the guard office for a purpose. He not only loved the Christians in East Berlin but He loved these Communist guards also – the officer and the uniformed typist. What a sad mistake we sometimes make when we think that God only cares about Christians. Although God desires that all people become Christians, He does not love one group more than another. In fact, it was for the world that God gave His only begotten Son, and Jesus Himself

112

said He had not come to call the righteous but sinners to repentance (*See* Matthew 9:13). I remembered the words of Jesus when He said, 'You will be led before kings and governors for My name's sake. This will be a time, an opportunity, for you to bear testimony. Resolve and settle it in your minds, not to meditate and prepare beforehand how you are to answer.' (*See* Matthew 10:18, 19.)

Suddenly my attitude towards the officer changed. Instead of an enemy, I saw him as one of those for whom Christ died. Now I answered every question testifying of my faith in Jesus. It became almost a kind of game.

I asked the officer, 'Did you ever read the Bible?'

'No, I am a Marxist,' he said stubbornly.

'The Bible was written especially for Marxists,' I said. 'It says that God so greatly loved the Marxists that He gave His only begotten Son so that any Marxist who believes in Him shall not perish, but have eternal life.'

Both the officer and the woman typist were listening with serious faces. I went ahead to talk about the two problems of the human race — sin and death — and stated that the Bible gives us the answer to these problems by telling us about Jesus.

'Why don't you keep my books and read them?' I said. 'I will be glad to autograph my book for you and the book by Billy Graham will answer many of your questions.'

'Must I read it?' the officer said.

'It will not do you any harm,' I laughed.

The officer laughed too, but then, catching himself, became very serious and businesslike again.

'I see, Fraulein, that you are carrying chocolate with you? What is your reason?'

'I am taking it for the minister's children in East Berlin. Don't you bring chocolate with you when you visit a family with children?'

'No, I take flowers with me,' he said seriously.

'Flowers are nice for parents, but children prefer chocolate. Besides, I often preach about chocolate.'

'What crazy people we have here today,' the officer said. 'You carry books by a man who talks like a machine gun and then tell me you preach about chocolate. Tell me, what kind of sermon do you get from a chocolate bar, old woman?'

'Several years ago,' I answered, 'I spoke to a group of Germans who prided themselves as intellectuals. They would not receive me because they felt that they were more profound in their theology than I. So, my last time with them I brought them all some Dutch chocolates. Since chocolate was very rare after the war, they eagerly accepted my gift. Later, when I stood to speak to them, I told them, "No one has said anything to me about the chocolate."

'They disagreed, saying that they had all thanked me for it.

' "I did not mean that," I said. "I mean no one questioned me about it. No one asked whether it had been manufactured in Holland or Germany, what quantities it contained of cocoa, sugar, milk, or vitamins. Instead of analysing it, you just ate it."

'Then I picked up my Bible and said, "It is the same with this Book. If you try to analyse it as a book of science or even a book of theology, you cannot be nourished by it. Like chocolate, it is to be eaten and enjoyed, not picked apart bit by bit." '

I stopped talking and noticed, once again, that the officer and the typist were deeply interested in what I was saying. Then the officer straightened up, cleared his throat, and said to the typist, 'Please type Fraulein ten Boom's protocol and we will let her pass.' With that he stood and left the room, never looking back.

I sat quietly while the typist finished typing her report.

Moments later the officer was back. He pulled the paper from the typewriter and read aloud. 'When in prison Corrie ten Boom received from God the commission to bring the Gospel of Jesus Christ over the whole world. Her church has taught her to bring chocolate when she visits families with children.'

The officer nodded and excused himself, saying he had to read it to his superior officer before I could be approved for entrance into East Berlin. While he was gone I talked with the typist, urging her to accept Jesus as her Lord. She listened intently, reading through some of the pages in my book. However, when the officer returned she straightened up and returned to her typewriter.

I handed Billy Graham's book to the officer. 'Sir, be sure and take this book by God's Machine Gun home with you. It will change your life.'

He tried to look severe, but behind his eyes I could sense both hunger and thirst. Without saying a word he took the book and slipped it into his briefcase. He handed my book to the typist and motioned her to put it in her purse. Then he opened the door and pointed in the direction of East Berlin. 'I am sorry to have detained you so long, Fraulein,' he said. 'But what we have been doing here is even more important than your visit to your friends.'

I shook his hand and Conny and I entered the Communist city, wondering if the officer actually realized the truth of his last statement. What we had to do in East Berlin was important, but even more important was bringing the Good News of Jesus to those who walk in darkness.

If you are reproached for being Christ's followers, that is a great privilege, for you can be sure that God's Spirit of glory is resting upon you.

1 Peter 4:14 PHILLIPS

17 Facing Death

Watchman Nee once said, 'When my feet were whipped my hands suffered pain.'

Christians all over the world are bound together as the body of Christ. Many Americans, in particular, do not realize it, but a part of that body is suffering the most terrible persecution and tribulation in the history of mankind. If we are members of that same body — and we are — then we must suffer with them, pray for them, and where it is possible, help them.

I remember hearing of a missionary — a single woman — who turned her back on all her possessions at home and went to China. 'Are you not afraid?' a friend asked as she prepared to board the ship. 'I am afraid of only one thing,' she said, 'that I should become a grain of wheat not willing to die.'

How much more like Christ that is than the churches who gather at Thanksgiving to sing:

Let thy congregation escape tribulation!

Several years ago I was in Africa in a little country where

an enemy had taken over the government. There was great oppression against the Christians by the new government. The first night I was there some of the native Christians were commanded to come to the police station to be registered. When they arrived they were arrested and during the night they were secretly executed. The next day the same thing happened with other Christians. The third day it was the same. By that time the entire district realized that the Christians were being systematically murdered. It was the intent of the new government to eradicate them all — men, women, and children — much as Hitler tried to eradicate all the Jews.

I was to speak in a little church on Sunday morning. The people came, but I could see fear and tension written on every face. All during the service they looked at each other, their eyes asking the same questions: 'Will this one I am sitting beside be the next one to be killed? Will I be the next one?'

I looked out on that congregation of black and white faces. The room was hot and stuffy. Moths and other insects came through the screenless windows and swirled around the naked light bulbs hanging over the bare, wooden benches upon which the natives sat. They were all looking at me, expecting, hoping, that I could bring them a word from God for this tragic hour.

I opened my Bible and read 1 Peter 4: 12 – 14 (PHILLIPS):

And now, dear friends of mine, I beg you not to be unduly alarmed at the fiery ordeals which come to test your faith, as though this were some abnormal experience. You should be glad, because it means you are called to share Christ's sufferings. One day, when he shows himself in full splendour to men, you will be filled with the most tremendous joy. If you are reproached for being Christ's followers, that is a great privilege, for you can be sure that God's Spirit of glory is resting upon you.

I closed the Book and began to talk, simply, as an aunt would talk to her nieces and nephews. 'When I was a little girl,' I said, 'I went to my father and said, "Daddy, I am afraid that I will never be strong enough to be a martyr for Jesus Christ."

' "Tell me," Father said, "when you take a train trip from Haarlem to Amsterdam, when do I give you the money for the ticket? Three weeks before?"

' "No, Daddy, you give me the money for the ticket just before we get on the train."

' "That is right," my father said, "and so it is with God's strength. Our wise Father in heaven knows when you are going to need things too. Today you do not need the strength to be a martyr; but as soon as you are called upon for the honour of facing death for Jesus, He will supply the strength you need — just in time." '

I looked out at my African friends. Many of them had already lost loved ones to the firing squad or the headman's axe. I knew that others would surely die that week. They were listening intently.

'I took great comfort in my father's advice,' I said. 'Later I had to suffer for Jesus in a concentration camp. He indeed gave me all the courage and power I needed.'

My African friends were nodding seriously. They, too, believed God would supply all their needs, even the power to face death bravely.

'Tell us more, Tante Corrie,' one grizzled old black man said. It was as though they were storing up all the truth they could so they could draw on it in the day of trial.

I told them of an incident that had taken place in the concentration camp at Ravensbruck. 'A group of my fellow prisoners had approached me, asking me to tell them some Bible stories. In the concentration camp the guards called the Bible *das Lügenbuch* — the book of lies. Cruel death punishment had been promised for any prisoner who was found possessing a Bible or talking about the Lord. However, I went to my little cot, found my Bible, and returned to the group of prisoners.

'Suddenly I was aware of a figure behind me. One of the prisoners formed the words with her lips, "Hide your Bible. It's Lony." I knew Lony well. She was one of the most cruel of all the *aufseherinen* — the women guards. However, I knew that I had to obey God who had guided me so clearly to bring a Bible message to the prisoners that morning. Lony remained motionless behind me while I finished my teaching and then I said, "Let's now sing a hymn of praise."

'I could see the worried, anxious looks on the faces of the prisoners. Before it had been only me speaking. Now they, too, were going to have to use their mouths to sing. But I felt God wanted us to be bold, even in the face of the enemy. So — we sang.

'When the hymn was finished I heard a voice behind me. "Another song like that one," she said. It was Lony. She had enjoyed the singing and wanted to hear more. The prisoners took heart and we sang again — and again. Afterwards I went to her and spoke to her about the Lord Jesus Christ. Strangely, her behaviour began to change until, in a crude sort of way, she became a friend.'

I finished my story and stood silently while the words took their effect on my African friends. 'Let me tell you what I learned from that experience,' I told them. 'I knew that every word I said could mean death. Yet never before had I felt such peace and joy in my heart as while I was giving the Bible message in the presence of mine enemy.

God gave me the grace and power I needed — the money for the train ticket arrived just the moment I was to step on the train.'

The faces before me broke into broad grins. Gone were the wrinkles of fear and anxiety. Once again their eyes were flashing with joy and their hearts were filled with peace. I closed the service by reading a poem by Amy Carmichael.

> We follow a scarred Captain,
> Should we not have scars?
> Under His faultless orders
> We follow to the wars.
> Lest we forget, Lord, when we meet,
> Show us Thy hands and feet.

The meeting was over and the Africans stood to leave. Then softly, in the back of the room, someone began singing an old gospel song.

> There's a land that is fairer than day,
> And by faith we can see it afar.
> For the Father waits over the way,
> To prepare us a dwelling place there.
> In the sweet by and by, we shall meet on that beautiful
> shore.
> In the sweet by and by, we shall meet on that beautiful
> shore.

I don't know how many were killed that week, but someone told me that more than half those who had attended that service met a martyr's death — and thus received a martyr's crown. But I know that God's Spirit of glory had been resting upon them. (*See* 1 Peter 4:14.)

18   Saved by a Newborn Infant

One of my greatest privileges is visiting with missionaries all over the world. Those of us who live in the comfort and security of our homes cannot begin to imagine what the life of a missionary is like. Many of them have no fresh water and only simple food. They constantly face the threat of sickness and infection. Some live in primitive places where their very lives are in danger. Much to my sadness, yet to the glory of God, the list is growing longer each day of men and women who are literally laying down their lives for Jesus' sake on the mission field. These men and women stand on the front lines, often in lonesome places, but knowing that their Master who has placed them there will also stand with them.

Once in a primitive spot in Africa I visited a missionary couple. Their small home was located in a delightful spot that gave a beautiful view of lakes and mountains. They had very little of this world's goods, but were rich in God's grace and had been given a homesite that many wealthy people would pay thousands of dollars to have as their own. Crowded into this tiny shack were six children, the youngest just a few months old. 'Come with me,' the missionary wife said as she picked up the baby and walked outside. 'I want to tell you a story.'

We sat on a bench overlooking an awesome scene of grandeur. Spreading before us was a mighty view of the mountains, covered with deep jungle and spotted with lakes and waterfalls.

'To have many little children can be a burden for a missionary,' she said. 'There comes a time when you have to send them to the homeland because there are no good schools here. But while they are small you try to enjoy them.'

She paused and looked down at the sweet baby asleep in her arms. Her voice was tense with emotion as she continued. 'But when I learned I was going to have another baby, I rebelled against God. We already had five small children and it did not seem fair that we should have to bear another. My health was not good and I looked upon having another child with great sorrow and unhappiness.'

Tears were streaming down her face as she talked. 'Was it not enough to have five children? Oh, how my heart cried out at God and there were times when I wished He would take the baby from me.

'The time for the birth was here. I was very weak and there were no doctors nearby. We had no one to leave the other children with, so my husband put us all in the car and drove us into a town where there was a good mission hospital. There we stayed until the baby was born.'

The tiny child stirred in her arms, stretched her little arms and yawned. How precious she looked! The mother's voice grew soft. 'When we returned to our house with the new baby we learned that in the short days we had been gone the dreaded Mau Mau had come. They had murdered every white person in the entire area. Had we been home we would have all been killed.'

She hugged the little baby to her breast, tears flowing down her face. 'This little darling was sent by God to save all our lives. Never again shall I rebel against His ways for our lives.'

My times are in thy hand . . .

Psalms 31:15

19 Miracles Every Day

It was my first time in India and I was to speak at a conference of missionaries in Vellore. However, when my plane arrived in Bangkok I was told the next plane to Vellore did not leave for three days.

'But this means I will have to miss the first three days of the conference,' I said.

'We are sorry, but there is no way,' the man at the ticket counter told me. However, the airlines did make arrangements for me to stay at a hotel until the next plane left.

Arriving at the hotel I asked the kindly Indian man who was in charge of my arrangements, 'Is there no possibility that I can catch another plane to Vellore?'

'The airlines are making every effort,' he assured me.

'Then we must pray that God will help them,' I said.

'Do you *profess* to be a Christian?' he asked with a startled look on his face.

'Yes, I do,' I answered. 'I am a *professor* of Jesus Christ. And what about you?'

He hung his head. 'I have been, but I am what you call a lost sheep.'

'Hallelujah!' I said. 'Then you are just the one sheep for whom the Shepherd left the ninety-nine to find.'

We talked a long time in the lobby of the hotel. Finally I asked the man if he would be willing to come back to Jesus. 'Oh, yes,' he said. 'For I believe God kept you here just for this reason.'

We prayed together in the hotel and then I said to him, 'Now that God has used me for this miracle will you pray with me for another miracle — that I might arrive in Vellore in time for the conference?'

The man leaped to his feet. 'While you pray I must run an errand. I'll be back shortly.' With that he was out of the door, leaving me sitting among my suitcases.

Half-an-hour later he was back. 'Make quickly ready for the plane,' he said. 'I think God has performed your miracle. We have discovered another plane going by a different route to Vellore.'

'Did you arrange that?' I asked.

'I did,' he smiled as he hoisted my bags to his back. 'But don't thank me. I must thank you for bringing me back to the Shepherd.'

We rushed madly to the airport and I found the plane was supposed to have left long before. However, they were holding it just for me. Panting, I climbed the steps to the plane.

'Ah, Professor,' the stewardess said as she closed the door behind me, 'we were afraid we would have to leave you.'

'Professor?' I asked. 'What's this?'

'Oh,' she smiled sweetly. 'We know all about you. Our hotel agent told us that you are an important *professor* from Holland who has to give significant speeches in Vellore. That is why we have held the plane on the ground until you arrived.'

I took my seat near a window. Outside the once-lost sheep was grinning and waving. I waved back. *Surely*, I thought,

God not only had a special reason for keeping me in Bangkok, but He must have an equally important reason for wanting me in Vellore.

I was right. My first talk to the missionary conference in Vellore was the next morning. I spoke on the reality of God's promises in the Bible. After the service I slipped away from the crowd and strolled in a beautiful garden near the conference centre. It was alive with colour: green and red crotons mixed their rich colours with the dark orange of the copper plants and the rainbow hues of the flowering shrubs. *How wonderful*, I thought, *to be in the centre of God's will.*

'Excuse me,' a shy voice said from behind.

I turned and recognized one of the English missionary ladies. Her body seemed weak. She hesitated to speak but at last said, 'Do you really believe in God's promises?'

'Yes, I do,' I said.

'Do you believe the Lord still heals the sick?'

'Of course,' I answered. I motioned for her to sit with me on a stone bench near a flowering hibiscus. First I read to her from the Bible where Jesus said we would lay hands on the sick and they would be healed (*See* Mark 16:18–20). Then I told her of a recent experience in Indonesia.

'I was staying in the house of a dear Chinese pastor and his wife,' I said. 'Since we were so busy the wife had no time to cook, so a member of their church, another Chinese lady, came every day in a rickshaw to fix me a good Chinese meal.

'One morning I was sitting in the house and looked out of the window. I saw this dear woman stumbling up the pathway. Her head was bleeding and her dress badly torn. I rushed out to meet her and helped her into the house. Her rickshaw had collided with another rickshaw and she had been

126

badly injured, hitting her head against a metal part of the primitive vehicle. Since Chinese people were not popular in Indonesia at that time, no doctor would come to see her. Instead they just brought her to the house and let her out.

'I knew her condition was serious and also knew that the doctor would not come to the Chinese pastor's house either. Therefore, I just laid my hands on her and prayed in Jesus' Name that she be healed. She was restored instantly.'

The missionary lady was listening intently. 'Must you know a person's type of sickness before you pray for them?' she asked.

'No, I'm not a doctor. I do not heal. It is the Lord who heals.'

'I am very ill,' she said quietly. 'Will you lay hands on me and pray?'

'I will,' I said. She slipped off the bench and knelt in that beautiful garden while I put my hands on her head and prayed for her to be healed in the Name of Jesus Christ.

She rose slowly to her feet. 'Now I will tell you my sickness,' she said. 'I have leprosy.'

I had been in leper colonies and suddenly I was filled with great fear. *Oh*, I thought, *this is far too difficult for the Lord. I wish now she had told me ahead of time so I would have known not to pray for her.*

Then I felt ashamed and asked forgiveness for my small faith and unbelief. After all, it was not I who said He would heal the sick — but He who had said it.

Some years passed and I lost the name and address of the lady missionary, although many times I remembered that time in the garden and continued to pray for her. Five years later I was back in India, staying with friends of the Pocket Testament League. One afternoon there was a knock at my hotel door. 'Do you remember me?' a beautiful lady asked.

127

I looked at her and said, 'I have seen you before but I do not remember who you are.'

'Do you remember a time in Vellore when you laid hands on a leper patient and prayed in Jesus' Name that she be healed?'

'Oh, yes,' I exclaimed. 'I surely remember you. But you are a different person.'

She smiled. 'The Lord wonderfully healed me. The doctors say I am absolutely healed from leprosy.'

'Thank You, Lord,' I said aloud. 'Your Name be glorified! You are always ready to meet our needs, even when our faith is small.'

*The grass withereth, the flower fadeth: but
the word of our God shall stand for ever.*

Isaiah 40:8

20 God's Word, the Sword — God's Perfect Weapon

It had been a hectic half year. I had flown from New Zealand to Korea where I had spoken in more than two hundred and fifty meetings in a three-month period. I then returned to Hamilton, New Zealand, for a brief visit before continuing to India.

In New Zealand I had stayed with a family who were memorizing verses of Scripture, using the Navigators' system. I was thrilled to find so many of the new converts in New Zealand studying this course. Since I knew less Scripture in English than I did in Dutch, I, too, determined to start memorizing Scripture. I knew that once the Word of God was hidden in my heart it would be with me always.

Leaving New Zealand full of new zeal, I arrived in the state of Kerala, India, where I was to speak in a series of small conferences far back in the jungle. My Indian companion met me at the airport and took me to a small place on the river where a canoe was waiting. We climbed in and started our slow trip down the peaceful river. Slowly our little craft glided over the shallow waters. Except for the rhythmic sound of the paddle and the occasional murmur of the soft wind in the trees there was nothing to be heard.

My Indian companion was the leader of a home group. Twice a year the home groups in the area come together in a conference to study the Bible, pray, and plead for revival. I was to speak three times a day in several such conferences which would be held in a *pandal* — a wide roof protecting the congregation from the hot sun. There are no walls so the breeze may pass through and the people sit on the grassy floor.

As the coolie paddled our canoe down the river, my Indian companion told me of the great longing in his heart to win souls for Jesus Christ.

'Yet I am not successful,' he said. 'I always give my testimony, but I am not able to persuade people to make a decision.'

'Do you use the Sword of the Spirit, the Word of God?' I asked him.

'I fear I am not very adept at handling that Sword,' he admitted. 'Just at the critical moment I am never able to find a text that fits the situation.'

'Yes, I can understand that,' I confessed. 'I sometimes have the same problem. However, I am now memorizing certain verses of Scriptures which I call my First Aid Course. These are emergency Scriptures which I apply to the wound until I can look up the rest of the Scriptures which will bring further healing.'

My Indian companion brightened and then I told him of a recent experience in Canada where I had learned that it was not me, but the Word of God coming through me, that won people to Christ anyway.

'I had just finished speaking to a class of university students,' I told him as the canoe glided down the quiet river. 'I was relaxing on the veranda of one of the dormitories when a very educated woman, who had attended my lectures, sat down with me.

' "What you just told the students was very interesting," she said. "But you are too narrow. I am an expert on world religions. I have travelled to many countries and have had long discussions with the leaders of many religious groups. I have discussed the road of life through time and eternity with Muslims, Brahmins, Shintoists, and many others. All of them know God, even though they do not believe in Jesus Christ. I am sorry to have to disagree with your talk this afternoon, but you put too much emphasis on Jesus Christ and do not allow that other religions are just as good as Christianity."

'I was embarrassed,' I told my Indian companion. Then I remembered something a friend had once told me. "You are not called to convince anyone," he had said. "You are simply called to be an open channel for the Spirit of God to flow through. You can never be anything else, even though you may think so at times. Follow the pathway of obedience, let the Word of God do its own work, and you will be used by God far beyond your own powers."

'Therefore, I said to the woman, "Your argument is not with me, but with the Bible. It is not I who say these things, it is the Word of God. Jesus said that no man can come to the Father but by him. (*See* John 14:6.) If you wish to dispute someone, dispute Him." '

I looked at my Indian friend. His eyes were fixed on my face as he drank in what I was saying. I continued with the story. 'Some time later a reception was held in Ottawa, Canada, for all who wished to meet Prince Bernhard of the Netherlands. It was a pleasure to see so many Hollanders together. The prince looked tired, but he was cheerful and kind to us all. I met many old acquaintances and then, suddenly, I was face-to-face with this same lady who had so adamantly disputed with me some time before.

' "I am glad to see you," she said genuinely. "I have never

been able to forget what you said when you spoke at our university when you quoted Jesus, 'No man cometh unto the Father but by me.' I have tried to argue with that from every angle, but am unable to get away from the fact that Jesus said it. I can argue with you, but I am having a difficult time arguing with Him."

' "How wonderful," I told her. "Now you are listening to the voice of God. Keep listening. He has much more to say to you."

' "Yes," she said. "I believe He does."

'We parted and I have not seen her since, but I know the Sword of the Spirit is still doing its work in her life.'

I turned and looked at my Indian friend. He was nodding his head in understanding. 'If we diligently read the Bible, the Holy Spirit will give us the right words and Scripture references,' I said. 'If we depend on Him, we are like the branches of these vines along the river which bear fruit. However, if the branches are broken off, then no fruit will appear.'

By this time the forest had thinned out on either side of the river. We could see narrow paths which permitted the people to tread single file through the trees. It was almost dark and I saw, coming down the paths, files of Indian people carrying torches of lighted palm leaves in their hands. The white clothes they wore gave the scene a strange, ethereal appearance as though they were pilgrims walking to heaven. Many had gathered already in the *pandal* away in the distance and were singing a gospel song in a monotone, chanting it over and over as the white-robed pilgrims made their way to the meeting place.

After the meeting that night I lay in my little thatched hut, praising God for the power of the Word of God which had not only drawn these people together, but which had won them to the Lord Jesus Christ. In my mind I listed five reasons why I believe the Bible is inspired:

(1) It says so. '... holy men of God spake as they were moved by the Holy Ghost' (2 Peter 1:21).
(2) The effect it has upon all who believe and follow it.
(3) Though some of it was written more than two thousand years before Jesus arrived on earth, yet all the writers agree.
(4) The authors do not offer any excuses for their own faults or sins.
(5) The writers record some of the most harrowing scenes which affected them greatly, yet they never express one word of emotion. The Holy Spirit wanted the facts recorded, and not their feelings about the facts.

Many persons make the mistake of thinking they can measure the certainty of their salvation by their feelings. It is the Word of God that is their foundation and therefore it is essential for the new convert in Christ to have a practical knowledge of the Bible. More than anyone else it is the new convert who will come under the fire of the enemy. He needs the knowledge of the Sword of the Spirit. As the Lord Jesus used this Sword to overcome the evil one in His temptation experiences, so we must learn to defend ourselves against every sort of attack.

> *But lay up for yourselves treasures in heaven*
> *.... For where your treasure is, there will*
> *your heart be also.*
>
> Matthew 6:20, 21

21 Where Is Heaven?

Happiness is not dependent on happenings, but on relationships in the happenings.

My father taught me this when I was just a child. He often told me of the early days of his marriage. He had opened a small jewellery store in a narrow house in the heart of the Jewish section of Amsterdam. Poor Mother! She had dreamed of a home with a little garden. She loved beautiful things and spacious views. 'I love to see the sky,' she often said. Instead, she found herself on a narrow street, in an old house — the kind with only a single room on each story — with worn-out furniture which they had inherited from Grandmother. Yet they were both happy, not because of the circumstances but because of the relationships in the circumstances.

There, in Amsterdam in that narrow street in the ghetto, they met many wonderful Jewish people. They were allowed to participate in their sabbaths and in their feasts. They studied the Old Testament together and, on occasion, even the New Testament.

I have remembered, many times, the lessons I learned from my father about happiness and happenings. But never was it so clear as when I was in Korea, many, many years later.

I had been in the Orient for three months, spending much of the time in Korea. While there I spoke in many meetings in schools, orphanages, children's homes, and churches. One day, after I had spoken in a university, a theological student came to me. I had never seen such gloom on the face of a man who said he wanted to be a minister of the risen Christ.

'Why is it that you are so full of unhappiness?' I asked.

'I have lost my way,' he said sadly. 'When I first became a Christian my pastor taught me the Bible is true. In those days I had great happiness. But now I am studying the famous scholar, Rudolph Bultmann, who says our Bible is full of myths and fables. I have lost my way and no longer know where heaven is.'

I was angry. It did not seem right that the simple boys of Korea had to struggle through this horrible theology. They studied many hours at the universities, going to school twice as long as students in America, yet because of what they studied, they often lost their faith. I answered his question about heaven by telling him what I had just seen and heard the day before while driving through the countryside.

There I saw the poorest shack I had ever seen. It was a tiny lean-to, made from materials collected from the garbage heap — pieces of cardboard, tin cans which had been smashed flat, old boards ... As we drove past, though, I heard the beautiful voice of a woman singing. Seldom, even in the concert halls of Europe, had I heard such a sweet voice. We stopped the car and listened, for it was like the song of a skylark.

I said to the missionary who was travelling with me, 'Do you know that song?'

'Yes,' she said, 'it says, *Where Jesus is, 'tis heaven there.*'

135

Oh, how my heart leaped for joy as I heard this beautiful song coming from such a poor place. It is one thing to hear such a song in a dignified church, or pouring through the speakers of an expensive stereo set. But when one hears it coming from the poorest shack in the midst of such poverty, then it means something else.

I looked at the young theological student before me. 'Jesus said, "The Kingdom of heaven is within you" (Luke 17:21). Bultmann is wrong and Jesus is right. Heaven is not a myth or fairy story: heaven is a prepared place for prepared people. Theology in the hands of the Holy Spirit is a beautiful science. But in the hands of unbelievers it is death. If you want to find where heaven is, get out of your stuffy classroom and go back out into the countryside. Listen to the simple faith of those who read only the Bible and trust only in God, not in material things. What do they care if some theologian says that heaven is a fable. They have found Jesus, and where Jesus is, 'tis heaven there.'

And how shall they preach, except they be sent?

Romans 10:15

22 When You Are Tempted to Quit

The enemy tries to make everything work out for the worst. Usually it is not the big problems which depress me, but the multitude of inconveniences which stack up like small rocks to form an immovable mountain. Recently a series of such small incidents almost caused me to resign my commission from the Lord.

In my journeyings I often have to cross borders between countries. Knowing that smuggling is sin, I do not do it. My first irritation came through an encounter with a customs official.

'Do you have anything to declare?' he asked rudely.

'Yes,' I replied. 'Nylon stockings.'

I had put them on top of my luggage to show him, for I knew that at that time it was necessary to pay duty on such items.

'There are four pair here,' he said. 'You told me one pair.'

'No, I did not!' I answered.

But he did not believe me. For the next hour he searched my baggage. He tried all the little boxes to see if they had false bottoms. He squeezed my tooth-paste tube to see if it contained diamonds. He checked my shoes for false heels which might contain drugs. He felt the hem of my dresses to see if I had sewn pearls into them. He almost pulled the lining out of my suitcases. Of course he found nothing at all and finally allowed me to pass – after paying the duty on the four pair of stockings. I was both offended and unhappy.

Later I understood why this incident had made me so upset. I had not surrendered my self-righteousness. I was so sure of my own honesty that I suffered from the conse-quence of wounded pride. It is easier to surrender one's sins than one's virtues!

Unaware of the reason for my depression, I then dis-covered that I had missed my plane connections due to the delay in the customs office. I was forced to sleep on a couch in the ladies' room at the airport. However, I am a good sleeper and enjoyed a sound slumber. When I awoke, the amazed cleaning woman (who was sweeping the floor around my couch) said with admiration, 'How wonderful to be able to sleep so soundly with so much noise going on around you.'

Eventually the plane on which I was travelling flew into a storm making me feel airsick. Then the night following my arrival there was an earthquake. I hate earthquakes for they remind me of the bombs that fell during the war.

Then the kind people who should have arranged my meet-ings greeted my arrival with, 'We thought you needed a holi-day and rest so we have not organized anything.' Sometimes this is God's plan, but more often is it just a sign of people's laziness to make preparation. So I did not appreciate the fact they had not arranged any meetings for me.

The final inconvenience — one which caused me almost to give up completely — had to do with my room. My hosts put me in a small room that had no writing table. Ordinarily this would not have disturbed me for I am used

138

to writing on my knee, but on top of everything else that had happened, I crumpled like the camel loaded with straw. I blew up.

The reason was not hard to find. Self-pity had come into my heart. Self-pity is a nasty sin and the devil uses it and always starts his talks with 'Poor Corrie.'

This time he began by saying, 'Why must you always live out of your suitcases? Stay at home and then you won't have trouble with customs officials, passports, luggage, plane connections, and other things. Every night you will be able to sleep in the same comfortable bed; and there are no earthquakes in Holland. After all, you are no longer young. You've lived like a tramp for many, many years. It is time to hang up your harness and retire into a nice green pasture. Let someone else do the work. You've earned your reward.'

By this time I was nodding. 'Yes, yes, Satan, you are right.' So, having listened to his advice I wrote a friend in Holland who managed an international guest house where at the time I had a room kept for me with my own few pieces of furniture.

'I believe the time has now come for me to work in Holland,' I wrote. 'I am tired of all this travelling and I cannot stand having wheels beneath me any longer. Will you arrange to have a desk — a big one — put in front of the window in my room; and an easy chair — a very easy one — on the right ...' In my fantasy I had worked out a lovely dream of heaven here on earth, and me in the middle of it!

That afternoon I posted the letter and then came back to my room to look over my calendar. I jotted down all the names of people I would have to write, cancelling my appointments. Everyone would understand. Had not many said, 'My, you must be tired at your age!'?

Everything would have gone all right (or perhaps I should be truthful and say 'all wrong') had I not picked up my Bible. This old, black Bible has been my guidebook in times of light and in times of darkness. I began to read, asking, 'Lord, what would You have me do?'

I opened to the Book of Romans, chapter 10. 'How shall they call on Him in whom they have not believed? And how shall they believe in Him of whom they have not heard? And how shall they hear without a preacher? ... As it is written, how beautiful are the feet of them that preach the Gospel of peace, and bring glad tidings of good things.' (*See* verses 14, 15.)

I remembered the words of a paratrooper instructor. He said that when he had his men in the plane and they were over the battlefield he gave four commands.

FIRST   Attention! *Lift up your eyes* (John 4:35).

SECOND   Stand in the door! *Look upon the fields, for they are white already to harvest* (John 4:35).

THIRD   Hook up! *Be ye filled with the Holy Spirit* (*See* John 20:22).

FOURTH   Follow me! *I will make you fishers of men* (Mark 1:17).

I sat for a long time — thinking. It is not our task to give God instructions. We are to simply report for duty.

I laid my Bible on the bed and picked up pen and paper. Balancing the pad clumsily on my knee I wrote my friend in Holland.

Forget about that last letter I wrote. I am not coming home to Holland. I refuse to spend the rest of my life in a pasture when there are so many fields to harvest. I hope to die in harness.

And so, dear brothers, I plead with you to give your bodies to God. Let them be a living sacrifice . . . .

Romans 12:1 LB

23 I'll Go Where You Want Me to Go, Dear Lord . . . but Not Up Ten Flights of Stairs

I had spoken that Sunday morning in a church in Copenhagen, Denmark, urging the people to present their bodies as living sacrifices to the Lord. I had said even though I was an old woman that I wanted to give myself completely to Jesus and do whatever He wanted me to do, go wherever He wanted me to go — even if it meant dying.

After the church time, two young nurses approached me. They invited me up to their apartment to have a cup of coffee. I was very tired. At almost eighty years of age I found that standing on my feet for long periods of time was beginning to be exhausting. The cup of coffee sounded good so I accepted their invitation.

But I was not prepared for the walk up to their apartment. Many of the houses in Copenhagen are old, high houses with no elevators. The nurses lived on the tenth floor of such a house and we had to walk up the steps.

'O Lord,' I complained as I looked up at the high building, 'I do not think I can make it.' But the nurses wanted me to come up so badly that I consented to try.

By the time we reached the fifth floor my heart was pounding wildly and my legs were so tired I thought they could not take another step. In the corridor of the fifth floor I saw a chair and pleaded with the Lord, 'Lord, let me stay here a time while the nurses go on up the stairs. My heart is so unhappy.'

The nurses waited patiently as I collapsed into the chair, resting. 'Why, O Lord, must I have this stair-climbing after this busy day of speaking?'

Then I heard God's voice, even louder than my pounding heart. 'Because a great blessing is waiting you, a work which will give joy to the angels.'

I looked up at the steps, towering above me and almost disappearing into the clouds. Perhaps I am leaving this earth to go to heaven, I thought. Surely that will give joy to the angels. I tried to count the steps. It seemed there were at least one hundred more to climb. However, if God said that the work would give joy to the angels, then I had to go. I rose from my chair and once again started trudging up the long flights of stairs, one nurse in front of me, the other behind me.

We finally reached the apartment on the tenth floor and on entering I found a room with a simple lunch already prepared on the table. Serving the lunch were the mother and father of one of the girls.

I knew there was only a short time and also knew that a blessing of some kind was waiting us. So, without many introductions, I started asking immediate questions.

'Tell me,' I asked the nurse's mother, 'is it long ago that you found Jesus as your Saviour?'

'I have never met Him,' she said, surprised at my question.

'Are you willing to come to Him? He loves you. I have travelled in more than sixty countries and have never found anyone who said they were sorry they had given their hearts to Jesus. You will not be sorry either.'

Then I opened my Bible and pointed out the verses about salvation. She listened intently. Then I asked them, 'Shall we now talk with the Lord?'

I prayed, then the two nurses prayed and finally the mother folded her hands and said, 'Lord Jesus, I know already much about You. I have read much in the Bible, but now I pray You to come into my heart. I need cleansing and salvation. I know that You died at the cross for the sins of the whole world and also for my sins. Please, Lord, come into my heart and make me a child of God. *Amen.*'

I looked up and saw tears of joy on the face of the young nurse. She and her friend had prayed so much for her parents and now the answer was given. I turned and looked at the father, who had sat quietly through all this.

'What about you?' I asked him.

'I have never made such a decision for Jesus Christ either,' he said seriously. 'But I have listened to all you have told my wife and now I know the way. I, too, would like to pray that Jesus will save me.'

He bowed his head and from his lips poured a joyful but very sincere prayer as he gave his life to Jesus Christ. Suddenly the room was filled with great rejoicing and I realized the angels had come down and were standing around, singing praises unto God.

'Thank You, Lord,' I prayed as I walked back down the long steps, 'for making me walk up all these steps. And next time, Lord, help Corrie ten Boom listen to her own sermon about being willing to go anywhere You tell me to go — even up ten flights of stairs.'

For the earth shall be filled with the knowl-
edge of the glory of the Lord, as the waters
cover the sea.

Habakkuk 2:14

24   To All the World — Beginning With One

To give a tract to someone in Russia is always a risk. If the person you are talking to is alone, then there is a little more freedom. However, if a third person is present both are always uneasy — each afraid the other might turn him over to the secret police.

Conny and I had been in a Leningrad hotel for about a week when one morning, on our way down to breakfast, I handed the cleaning woman a tract. It was a simple tract, written in Russian, called 'The Way of Salvation'. It used only Scripture verses with no commentary.

She glanced at it and then glanced at the other woman cleaning the hall. She pushed the tract back to me, motioning with her hand as if to say, 'That is nothing for me.'

I felt sorry for her. The answer *no* hurts when you want to help someone. Conny and I continued on down the hall to the elevator, heading to the dining room for breakfast. We were the only ones on the elevator and on the way down I cast this latest burden on the Lord. 'Father, I can't reach this woman. Do bring her in contact with someone who can tell her the Gospel in her own language. Lord, I claim her soul for eternity.'

144

I was shocked by the boldness of my prayer. Never in all my life had I prayed that way. Was it proper? Could I actually claim the soul of someone else? In a kind of postscript I asked, 'Lord, was this wrong or right? May I say such a prayer?'

Then, even before I could receive His answer, I heard myself praying a prayer that frightened me even more. 'Lord Jesus, I claim all of Russia for You.'

The elevator stopped and Conny and I walked through the huge corridor to the dining room. I was bewildered. My cheeks were red and hot. 'Lord, was this right? Was this too much? But no, Lord, Your Word says, "The earth is the Lord's ... the world and they that dwell therein" (Psalms 24:1). Surely that means Russia, too.'

Still confused, we entered the dining room. It was crowded and the waiter came up and said, 'There are only two of you. You cannot eat breakfast here since all the tables are reserved for big groups.'

We looked around. A Japanese man had heard the waiter and motioned for us to come to his table where there were two empty places. 'Just come,' he said. 'We will act as if you belong to our group.'

But the waiter saw what had happened and refused to wait on us. I felt unhappy and unwelcome. Turning to Conny I said, 'At dinner yesterday I took some white buns up to my room in my purse. They are still there and we have some Nescafé. Why should we sit here and wait? Let us go to our room.'

It was quiet and peaceful upstairs. Our breakfast tasted good although it was only dry buns and Nescafé without any cream.

Suddenly there was a knock at the door. Conny opened it and there stood the cleaning woman, the one who had refused the tract. Her hair was pulled back in a tight bun and I noticed her heavy leather shoes squeaked when she walked. She closed the door behind herself. From her lips poured a stream of Russian words, not a single one of which we could understand. Then she pointed a finger at my brown bag.

'Conny, she wants to have a tract,' I almost shouted.

Conny gave her one but it was not the same one as we had given her the first time. She looked at it, shook her head, and pointed again at the bag.

'Conny, she wants to have "The Way of Salvation".'

I got up, rummaged through my bag, and found the original tract. I smiled and handed it to her. She looked at it and her face burst into a great light of joy. Smiling and nodding in appreciation, she backed out of the room.

I was beaming with joy too, for God had answered my prayer. I had not claimed too much after all. The first prayer had already been answered and now I was sure that the second prayer, the one the Holy Spirit had prayed through me without my first thinking up the words, was going to be given a *yes* answer, too.

Conny, who was as excited as I, took her Bible and read 'For the earth shall be filled with the knowledge of the glory of the Lord, as the waters cover the sea' (Habakkuk 2:14). What a promise — the whole of Russia under the waters of God's glory!

There was another knock at the door. There stood our cleaning woman again. She entered and put a long loaf of fresh white bread on the table. Her face was still wreathed in smiles as she refused payment for it. It was her thank offering to God.

I had never had such a good breakfast in all my life.

> *But I hold this against you, that you have left*
> *your first love.*
>
> *See* Revelation 2:4

25 Leaving My First Love

After twenty years of wandering the world as a tramp for
the Lord I was ill. At seventy-three years of age my body
had grown tired. A doctor examined me and said, 'Miss ten
Boom, if you continue at the same pace you cannot possibly
work much longer. However, if you will take a furlough
for a year then perhaps you can work for another few
years.'

I consulted my Lord. He said very clearly that this advice
of the doctor was in His plan. It came to mind that I could
live during that 'Sabbath Year' in Lweza, a beautiful house
in Uganda, East Africa. Several years before I had contributed to this place so it could be used as a house of rest for
missionaries and other workers in God's Kingdom. Now the
bread I had cast upon the waters was coming back to me. I
made my plans and soon Conny and I were safely ensconced
in Africa.

Lweza was a paradise. Built on a hill in the midst of a
garden that must surely resemble Eden, it looked southward
out over Lake Victoria. The climate was ideal. Since there
were many universities, churches, prisons, and groups in
Kampala, the nearby town, I was able to speak in two or

three meetings a week. So, while my body rested, my spirit remained active.

The greatest pleasure was to sleep every night in the same bed. During the last twenty years I had slept in more than a thousand different beds, always living out of my suitcases. This year I rested. I put my clothes in a drawer, hung my dresses in a closet, and best of all, each night I laid my head on the same pillow.

In November the Sabbath Year had gone by. Conny and I took a map of the world and stretched it out across my bed, following our usual method of making plans for the next year — the same method I had used for the last twenty years. First we listened to God's plan, then we signed it. This was unlike the method I once used when I made my own plans and then asked God to sign them. Our desire was to be 'planned' by the Holy Spirit.

God's plan looked very good to Conny. There would be three months in different countries in Africa, two months in America, and then three months in Eastern Europe behind the Iron Curtain. 'Thank You, Jesus,' Conny said. But inside I was not so thankful. Conny was young, much younger than I. She loved to travel but I was getting old and was still rather tired.

After Conny left I turned to the Lord. 'I prefer to stay here,' I said stubbornly. 'There is so much to do in Kampala and Entebbe, the two nearest cities. I will work for You. I am willing to have meetings every day, counselling, writing books; but please, let me sleep every night in the same bed. Everyone can understand that at my age I should take it a bit easier.'

I got up rejoicing. This new plan of mine made me really happy.

Then Conny called. An African minister from far away Ruanda had come to visit. He started immediately to welcome me: 'We are so glad that you are willing to come to Ruanda again. Five years ago you helped us so marvellously when you told what the Lord had been to you in your great need. You said that it was not your faith that helped you through three prisons, for your faith was weak and often wavering. You said it was the Lord Himself who carried you through and that you knew from experience that Jesus' light is stronger than the deepest darkness.'

The African brother continued, 'Five years ago, however, that was just theory to us. None of us had ever been prisoners. Now there has been a civil war in our country. Many of us have been in prison, I, myself, was in prison for two years. It was then that I remembered everything you had said. I did not have the faith of Corrie ten Boom, I did not even have faith for myself, but I knew to look to the same Jesus who gave you faith. He has also given it to me and that is why we are so happy that you are now coming again to Ruanda.'

But I was not happy at all. His words were different from what I wanted to hear. I knew that in such situations I could change the subject by asking a question. Perhaps this would make God stop reminding me of His plans and leave me alone so I could follow mine.

'How is the church in Ruanda?' I asked. 'What kind of message do they need now?'

Without hesitating one moment the brother opened his Bible and began to read:

Write this to the angel of the Church in Ephesus: These words are spoken by the one who holds the seven stars safe in his right hand, and who walks among the seven golden lampstands. I know what you have done; I know how hard you have worked and what you have endured ... I know your powers of endurance — how you have

149

suffered for the sake of my name and have not grown weary. But I hold this against you, that you [have lost your first love]. Remember then how far you have fallen . . .'

Revelation 2:1–5 PHILLIPS

This arrow penetrated my heart. Not only Ruanda needed that message, but also Corrie ten Boom. I had lost my first love. Twenty years before I had come out of a concentration camp — starved, weak — but in my heart there was a burning love: a love for the Lord who had carried me through so faithfully — a love for the people around me — a burning desire to tell them that Jesus is a reality, that He lives, that He is victor. I knew it from experience. For this reason I went to Germany and lived in the midst of the ruins. For this reason I had tramped the world for twenty years. I wanted everyone to know that no matter how deep we fall, the Everlasting Arms are always under us to carry us out.

And now? Now I was interested in my bed. I had lost my first love. I asked my African brother to continue to read.

Repent and live as you lived at first. Otherwise, if your heart remains unchanged, I shall come to you and remove your lampstand from its place.

Suddenly joy came in my heart. I could bring my sin, my cold heart, my weary body to Him who is faithful and just. I did it. I confessed my sins and asked for forgiveness. And the same thing happened that always happens when I bring my sin to God in the Name of Jesus: He forgave me. Jesus cleansed my heart with His blood and refilled me with the Holy Spirit.

As God's love — the fruit of the Holy Spirit — was

poured out into my heart, I set out again on my journeys — a tramp for the Lord.

What a great joy it was to experience the love of God, who gave me rivers of living water for the thirsty world of Africa, America, and Eastern Europe. Of course, it might be the will of God that some old people retire from their work. In great thankfulness to the Lord they can then enjoy their pensions. But for me, the way of obedience was to travel on, even more so than ever before.

Jesus warned us in Matthew 24:12 that the love of most men waxes cold because iniquity abounds. It is very easy to belong to the 'most men'. But the gate of repentance is always wide open. *Hallelujah!*

> *But if we walk in the light, as he is in the*
> *light, we have fellowship one with another,*
> *and the blood of Jesus Christ his Son cleanseth*
> *us from all sin.*
>
> 1 John 1:7

26 Walking in the Light

Our last few weeks in Lweza proved to be the most fruitful of our entire time spent there, for it was in these weeks that I learned another valuable lesson — the lesson of walking in the light.

One afternoon Conny and I were sitting in the garden looking at the monkeys jumping from one tree to another. The trees and shrubs were a mass of colour and sound, causing my heart to be filled with the glory of God's grace.

Yet Conny was discouraged. She had started a girl's club in the YWCA in Kampala and had spent many hours work with it. However, the girls were not interested. I was concerned about her discouragement, feeling it went far deeper than the problems she was having with her class.

I started to ask her about it when we were interrupted by a man walking towards our hill. Conny squinted her eyes into the sun and then shouted, 'It is William Nagenda!'

What a joy it was to meet that dear African saint again. I never met an African with whom I could laugh so much and yet learn so much at the same time.

After we exchanged greetings William said, 'When I saw

152

you sitting here together a question came to my mind, "Do they walk in the light together?" '

We answered almost simultaneously. 'Oh yes, we do walk in the light together. We are a team.'

Just at that moment a boy from the house called that there was a telephone message for me. I excused myself while Conny and William remained behind to talk.

Conny was sitting in a cane and wicker chair while William squatted on his haunches beside the path, his brown knees poking up beside his face.

'I have something to confess to you,' Conny said to William.

'And what is that?' he answered gently.

'Your question gripped my heart. I must tell you that I do not really walk in the light with Tante Corrie.'

William's face broke into a wide grin and his eyes began to sparkle. 'So, that is why God had me ask that strange question.'

Conny was serious. 'Tante Corrie is so much more mature than I,' she continued. 'She has walked with Jesus for so many years. She has suffered much for Him in many ways. Thus when I see things in her life that are not right, I hesitate to speak them out to her.'

'Oh,' William said, startled. 'That is not right. The Lord wants you to be very honest with Tante Corrie. That is one reason He has put you with her. Since she is walking in the light then when you also walk in the light, you will help shed light for her path as well as yours.'

That night, after we had gone to our room together, Conny sat on the side of the bed and said, 'Tante Corrie, this is very difficult for me to say, but I now realize I must walk in the light.'

I turned and looked at her. Her face was drawn and solemn. One by one she began listing the things in my life which bothered her — the things I did which she did not believe glorified God. It was not easy for me to hear the things which I had done wrong — things which had caused a shadow to come in Conny's heart. But how wonderful it was that Conny was being completely honest with me. I apologized for the things she had listed and then thanked her for bringing them into the light. 'Let us always walk in the light together,' I said seriously.

But it was still hard for Conny. She was much younger than I and felt she was still learning. Even though I wanted her to continue to correct me, she found it very difficult. The final breakthrough came after we left Africa and flew to Brazil.

We had been in Rio de Janeiro, one of the most beautiful cities of the world, for a few weeks. As we prepared to leave — to fly south to Buenos Aires — we discovered our suitcases were overweight. The kind people in Rio had given us so many presents we were more than twenty kilograms overweight. It was going to cost us a great deal of extra money to go on to Argentina.

I unpacked my luggage and made three piles: one to send to Holland by sea, one to give away to the poor in Rio, and the smallest one to go back in my suitcase to carry on to our next destination. Finishing my repacking I hurried next door into Conny's room and unpacked her suitcase also. I went through the same procedure, sorting her belongings into three heaps and then repacking only her necessary items. I was in too much of a hurry to notice that Conny said nothing.

A week later, after a beautiful time in Buenos Aires, we were walking along a lonely stretch of beach near our cabin. I was enjoying the beautiful view over a quiet bay when Conny began to talk. Her voice was strained. 'I promised God I would walk in the light,' she said, 'and that means that I must get something settled with you. When you re-packed my suitcase and decided what things to send to Holland and what to leave with me, I was not happy about it.'

How stupid and tactless I had been to rush in and interfere with Conny's life! I reached out and took her hand. 'How thoughtless I have been,' I said. 'Forgive me for not leaving it up to you.'

'I do forgive you,' Conny said. Like myself, she had learned not to play lightly with sin, but to hear another's apology and then, instead of passing it off, to forgive it. We walked on for a long time in silence and then Conny spoke again.

'Are you unhappy, Tante Corrie? You are so quiet.'

Now it was my time to walk in the light. 'There is something hindering me,' I said, 'Why did you not tell me immediately that you were disturbed? That way it could have been settled on the spot and you would not have had to carry this darkness for all these days. From now on let us both "speak the truth in love" and never let the sun go down on our misunderstandings.'

It was a good lesson. From then until Conny married in 1967 and went to live with her husband, we walked all over the world — always trying to walk in the light.

I say therefore to the unmarried and widows,
It is good for them if they abide even as I.

1 Corinthians 7:8

27   Secure in Jesus

It is Satan who tries, in every way, to spoil the peace and joy that God's servants have in their work.

Ellen, my new travelling companion, had gone with me to a lonely mission field in Mexico. Our hostess was a lady missionary, unmarried, in her forties. One evening while we were alone in her little adobe, she confessed her bitterness and resentment over being unmarried.

'Why have I been denied the love of a husband, children, and a home? Why is it that the only men who ever paid any attention to me were married to someone else?' Long into the night she poured out the poison of her frustration. At last she asked me, 'Why did you never marry?'

'Because,' I said, 'the Lord had other plans for me than married life.'

'Did you ever fall in love and lose someone, as I have?' she asked bitterly.

'Yes,' I said sadly. 'I know the pain of a broken heart.'

'But you were strong, weren't you,' she said in biting tones. 'You were willing to let God have His way in your life?'

'Oh, no, not at first,' I said. 'I had to fight a battle over it. I

156

was twenty-three. I loved a boy and believed he loved me. But I had no money and he married a rich girl. After they were married he brought her to me and putting her hand in mine said, "I hope you two will be friends." I wanted to scream. She looked so sweet, so secure and content in his love.

'But I did have Jesus, and eventually I went to Him and prayed, "Lord Jesus, You know that I belong to You one hundred per cent. My sex life is yours also. I don't know what plans You have for my life, but Lord, whatever it may be, use me to realize Your victory in every detail. I believe You can take away all my frustrations and feelings of unhappiness. I surrender anew my whole life to You." '

I looked across the little table at the bitter woman in front of me. Her face was furrowed, her eyes hard with resentment. I sensed she had been trying to run away from her frustrations. Perhaps that was even the reason she was on the mission field. Sadly, there are some of God's children who go to the mission field to escape the pain of not having a husband. I know others, back home, who spend every evening away from their families, attending Christian meetings, because they are unhappy and frustrated in their marriages. Work — even mission work — can become a wrong hiding place.

'Those called by God to live single lives are always happy in that state,' I said. 'This happiness, this contentment, is the evidence of God's plan.'

'But you loved and lost,' she exclaimed. 'Do you believe that God took away your lover to make you follow Him?'

'Oh, no,' I smiled. 'God does not take away from us. He might ask us to turn our backs on something, or someone, we should not have. God never takes away, however; God gives. If I reach out and take someone for myself and the Lord steps in between, that does not mean God takes.

Rather it means He is protecting us from someone we should not have because He has a far greater purpose for our lives.'

We sat for long minutes in the semi-dark room. Only a small kerosene lamp gave its flickering light, casting faint shadows on the walls and across our faces. I thought back — remembering. I had always been content in the Lord. Back when I was in my thirties God gave me children — the children of missionaries — whom I raised. Betsie, my sister, fed and clothed them while I was responsible for their sports and music. We kept them in our home in Holland, and I found deep satisfaction in seeing them grow to maturity. I also spent a great deal of time speaking and sharing in various clubs for girls. But it was not the work that brought balance to my life, for work cannot balance our feelings. It was because my life was centred in the Lord Jesus that I had balance. Many people try to lose their feelings in work, or sports, or music, or the arts. But the feelings are always there and will eventually, as they had done tonight in this missionary, come boiling to the surface and express their resentment and discontent.

I turned to Ellen, my companion. Ellen is a tall, blond, beautiful Dutch girl then in her early thirties. She is single, yet she has learned the secret of living a balanced life. While I believe God set me apart before I was born to live a single life, Ellen was different. She did not feel that God had called her to a single life; rather she felt that one day, in God's time, she would marry. However, until that time arrived — one year or thirty years from then — I knew she was secure in Jesus and was not looking to a husband or children for her security.

I spoke to the missionary. 'There are some like me, who are called to live a single life,' I said softly. 'For them it is always easy for they are, by their nature, contented. Others, like Ellen, are called to prepare for marriage which may come later in life. They, too, are blessed, for God is using the in-between years to teach them that marriage is not the answer to unhappiness. Happiness is found only in a balanced relationship with the Lord Jesus.'

'But it is so hard,' she said, tears welling up in her eyes.

'That is so,' I said. 'The cross is always difficult. "But you are dead, and your life is hid with Christ in God' (Colossians 3:3). Dear girl, it cannot be safer. That part of you which would cling to a husband is dead. Now you can move into a life where you can be happy with or without a husband — secure in Jesus alone.'

I do not know if she really understood me, for often we set our minds on some one thing we think will make us happy — a husband, children, a particular job, or even a 'Ministry' — and refuse to open our eyes to God's better way. In fact, some believe so strongly that only this thing can bring happiness, that they reject the Lord Jesus Himself. Happiness is not found in marriage; or work; or ministry; or children. Happiness is found by being secure in Jesus.

After these things the Lord appointed other
seventy also, and sent them two and two be-
fore his face into every city and place....

Luke 10:1

28   I Have Much People in This City

My second trip to Cuba was much different from the earlier
one because this time Cuba was in the hands of Communists. Ellen was with me and we had come from Mexico
with our bags loaded with books. Friends had told us
that the Communists in Cuba were burning Bibles and
confiscating Christian literature, so I was not at all sure if we
could be allowed to bring all these books in with us. We had
also heard that most of the churches were closed and many
of the Christians were in prison — some of them for passing
out literature. Thus we were very cautious.

At the customs, in Havana, the officer pointed to my suitcases. 'What are these books?' he asked.

'They are written by me,' I said. 'I am going to give them
to my friends.'

I saw him scowl as he picked one of them up. My heart
began to beat rapidly. 'Oh, Lord,' I prayed inwardly, 'what
must I do?'

Then I heard myself saying brashly, 'Would you like to
have one of my books? Here, I will autograph it especially
for you.'

The customs officer looked up. I took the book from his hand and wrote my name in the front and then handed it back. He grinned broadly and thanked me. Then, glancing once more at my suitcase filled with books, he nodded and motioned us through the line. I closed the suitcase and stepped out on the streets. Hallelujah! The miracle had happened.

But why were we here? What kind of plans did the Lord have for us on this island? Had all our former friends been put in prison? Were any of the churches still open? These and many other questions pounded at my mind as we turned our faces towards the city.

An Intourist limousine brought us into the heart of Havana where we found a hotel room. After washing up we went out on to the streets, hoping to find some Christians. But how do you find Christians in a strange city when you cannot even speak their language? We walked up and down the sidewalks, hoping God would show us someone to speak to, but we received no guidance whatsoever.

I finally approached an old man who was leaning against the side of the building. He had a kindly face, I thought. I asked if he knew where there was a church.

He shrugged his shoulders but then, motioning us to wait, went to one of the free telephones along the street. Ellen and I stood praying. Was he going to call the police? Had we broken a law and would we be put in jail? Then we realized he was calling some of his friends, asking if they knew the whereabouts of a church. No one knew anything and he returned, saying he could be of no help.

We were discouraged and to make matters worse, it started to rain. Neither Ellen nor I had a raincoat and soon we were soaked to the skin. We had been walking for hours and I was exhausted.

'Ellen, can we try to get a taxi?' I asked.

'Well, Tante Corrie, we will need a miracle. However, we know that all things are possible with God.'

I found a little stool and sat down while Ellen walked on down the street, hoping to find a taxi. I looked out over the sea and felt as if I had just waded out of the surf, so wet was I. I thought of the words of the driver of the Intourist limousine as he had brought us from the airport. 'This is the hospital,' he had said as we drove by. 'Everyone who is ill can go there and it does not cost a penny. Here is a cemetery. When you die, we bury you and even that does not cost your relatives anything.'

I had been in many countries, but this was the first place they had offered to bury me!

We knew that the Lord had sent us to Cuba, but we had no idea of our mission. Where were the churches? We had seen some, but they were closed. Some even had trees growing in front of the doors. We had tried to call some Christians, but the ones we knew were no longer living in the area. I sat, waiting, while the water poured down my face. Then I heard a car stopping in front of me. Looking up, I saw Ellen's face in the rear window of the ancient, rusted vehicle.

'Tante Corrie,' she called above the sound of the rain, 'here I am again.' I hobbled to the taxi and got in the back door. 'Be careful where you put your feet,' Ellen laughed, 'or you will touch the street.'

The taxi took us to our hotel and soon we were in dry clothes, our wet garments hung across the fixtures in the bathroom where the steady drip, drip of water reminded us of our failure out on the street. I love to walk with Jesus, but after eight decades I realized I was not as young as I used to be. It was in such moments that I started to feel old.

Ellen could not sleep that night. We were supposed to stay in Cuba for two weeks, but if we could not find any Christians then what would we do? She arose in the middle of the night and prayed, 'Lord, give me a word so I may know we aren't in this country in vain.'

Sitting on the side of her bed, she reached for her Bible which was on the small table. She began to read where she had stopped the night before. She had learned that God does not want His children to be fearful, and the best way to overcome fear is through the Word of God.

She read Acts 18:9, 10.

Then spake the Lord to Paul ... Be not afraid, but speak, and hold not thy peace. For I am with thee, and no man shall set on thee to hurt thee: for I have much people in this city.

What an answer!

The next morning Ellen could not wait to find all those people, and neither could I. She had one address which we had not contacted. It was the address of a small house on a side street where some Christians we had once known used to live. Walking from the hotel, she finally found the street and made her way to a dingy door, weatherbeaten and cracked. She knocked boldly.

A small man, deeply tanned and with wrinkles around his eyes, cautiously opened the door. Ellen could speak no Spanish, but she held up her Bible, and one of my books (*Amazing Love*) which had been translated into Spanish.

The man glanced at the books and then back to Ellen. Ellen smiled and pointed to my name on the book, then pointed back towards the city. Suddenly his whole face came alive. He threw open the door and shouted, 'Corrie! Corrie ten Boom *está aquí. Ella está en Havana*!'

Ellen walked in and found the room was filled with men, all kneeling on the floor. They were pastors who met each week to pray for God's help and guidance in their difficult ministry. Ellen hurried back to the hotel and soon I was meeting with these wonderful men of God. We distributed all our books and made many new friends among God's people. Indeed, God did have 'much people' in that city.

Cast thy bread upon the waters: for thou shalt
find it after many days.

Ecclesiastes 11:1

29 The Blessing Box

Many times, on my trips around the world, I am dependent
on the hospitality of Christians. From the time of my first
trip to America when I was befriended by God's people in
New York, and later by Abraham Vereide in Washington,
D.C., I have known the love and generosity of others in
the Body of Christ.

It was on one of those continual trips, when my only
home was my suitcase (that big red one), that I was invited to stay with friends in Colorado. I didn't feel well
and needed rest. My hostess escorted me to her lovely house
with tall white columns. Taking me up the carpeted stairs
she showed me to a beautiful room. From the windows I
could see the clear, blue sky which framed the snow-capped
Rocky Mountains. She then put her arms around me and
said, 'Corrie, this is your room. It will always be here for
you.'

'This room! For me?' I could hardly believe it was true.
A place for me to unpack my suitcase! To hang up my
clothes! To spread out my writing papers and put my Bible
on a desk! Since that grey time in the concentration camp
I had longed for bright colours, as a thirsty man yearns for

water. This room, and the scenery outside, was filled with colour. I wanted to cry, as a child cries when she is happy. But I have learned to control my tears (most of the time, anyway) and was content just to tell the Lord of my deep thankfulness. The Lord is so good for He has given me so many friends, just like this, all over the world.

It was during one of my visits in this Colorado home that I received an early morning telephone call. I was already awake since we intended to leave that afternoon to fly to Washington to speak in a series of meetings arranged by Mr. Vereide.

The phone call was from Alicia Davison, Mr. Vereide's daughter. 'Oh, Alicia, I cannot wait to see you today. I am looking forward to it and the meetings in your fellowship house.'

There was a pause, then Alicia said, 'Tante Corrie, Dad is with the Lord.'

'Oh, Alicia ...' I tried to speak, but nothing else would come out.

'It is all right, Tante Corrie,' she said calmly. 'I am calling to ask you to please come on to be with all of us. We will not have the meetings, but so many people are coming and we want you to be with us.'

'I shall be there this afternoon,' I said. After a brief prayer over the phone, I hung up.

I hurried to finish my packing, remembering all the kindnesses that had been poured on me by this wonderful family and their many friends. I have faced death many times, but there is always an empty place in my heart when someone I know and love leaves to be with the Lord. Nor did it ever occur to me that almost two years later I would once again fly to Washington to sit in that same Presbyterian Church not to attend a memorial for Abraham Vereide but to attend the meeting in honour of Alicia, who, although still young and beautiful, would die in Hong Kong while making a mission tour with her husband, Howard Davison.

I was warmly received by my friends in Washington. Although sad, they were rejoicing in the Lord. That night after I had gone to my room, I prayed. 'Lord,' I asked, 'Why are people so kind to me? I am just a simple old Dutch woman. Why am I treated so graciously and shown so much hospitality?'

Then the Lord reminded me of my mother's blessing box.

Our house in Haarlem was not really big but it had wide open doors.

I do not suppose that the many guests who were always coming to the Beje ever realized what a struggle it was to make both ends meet. Yet many lonesome people found a place with us and joined in our music, humour, and interesting conversation. There was always a place at the oval dinner table, although perhaps the soup was a bit watery when too many unexpected guests showed up. Our entire home was centred in the ministry of the Gospel. All people who came to us were either workers in the Kingdom of God or people who needed help.

Mother loved all her guests. She often showed her love by dropping a penny in the 'blessing box' when they arrived.

The blessing box was a small metal box that sat on the sideboard near the oval dinner table. Here money was collected for the mission that was so close to our hearts. Every time our family was blessed in a particular way, Mother would drop money in the blessing box as a thank offering to God. This was especially true if Father sold an expensive watch or received extra money for repairing an antique clock.

Whenever visitors came Mother would spread her arms wide and welcome them and then to show how she really appreciated their presence would say, 'A penny in the blessing box for your coming.' If it were a special visitor she might even put in a dime.

Then, at the dinner table, Father would always bless our visitors, thanking God that our house was privileged by their presence. It was always a special occasion for us all.

I well remember the sister-in-law of a minister who spent the night with us. The next morning Tante Anna went to her room and found her sheet twisted into a rope and lying across the bed.

'What is this?' Tante Anna asked.

The woman broke down in tears. 'I must confess. Last night I wanted to commit suicide. I made my sheet into a rope and tied it around my neck to jump from the window. But I could not forget the prayer at the dinner table, as Mr. ten Boom thanked God that I could come and share in this hospitality. God spared my life through that prayer.'

After a few days in Washington I continued my travelling as a tramp for the Lord. However, fresh on my mind was the hospitality of my dear friends. And I remembered Mother's blessing box, and Father's prayers. Often I am dependent on the hospitality of Christians. God's people have been so generous to open their homes to me and many times when I lay my head on a strange pillow, which has been blessed by the love of my friends, I realize that I am enjoying the reward for the open doors and open hearts of the Beje.

Heaven will be blessed, but here on earth I already am enjoying a 'house with many mansions'.

*If we confess our sins, he is faithful and just
to forgive us our sins, and to cleanse us from
all unrighteousness.*

1 John 1:9

30   Closing the Circle

It would seem, after having been a Christian for almost
eighty years, that I would no longer do ugly things that need
forgiving. Yet I am constantly doing things to others that
cause me to have to go back and ask their forgiveness. Sometimes these are things I actually do — other times they are
simply attitudes I let creep in which break the circle of God's
perfect love.

I first learned the secret of closing the circle from my
nephew, Peter van Woerden, who was spending the weekend
with me in our little apartment in Baarn, Holland.

'Do you remember that boy, Jan, that we prayed for?'
Peter asked.

I well remember Jan. We had prayed for him many times.
He had a horrible demon of darkness in his life and although we had fasted and prayed and cast out the demon in
the name of the Lord Jesus Christ, the darkness always returned.

Peter continued, 'I knew God had brought this boy to me
not only so he could be delivered, but to teach me some
lessons too.'

I looked at Peter. 'What could that boy, Jan, so filled with
darkness, teach you?'

'I did not learn the lesson from Jan,' Peter smiled. 'But from God. Once in my intercession time for Jan the Lord told me to open my Bible at 1 John 1:7–9. I read that passage about confessing our sin and asked the Lord what that had to do with the darkness in Jan's life.'

Peter got up and walked across the room, holding his open Bible in his hand. 'God taught me that if a Christian walks in the light then the blood of Jesus Christ cleanses him from all sin, making his life a closed circle and protecting him from all outside dark powers. But —' he turned and emphatically jabbed his finger into the pages of the Bible — 'if there is unconfessed sin in that life, the circle has an opening in it — a gap — and this allows the dark powers to come back in.'

Ah, I thought, *Peter has really learned a truth from the Lord.*

'Tante Corrie,' Peter continued, 'even though I was able to cast out the demon in Jan's life, it always crept back in through the opening in the circle — the opening of Jan's unconfessed sin. But when I led Jan to confess this sin, then the circle was closed and the dark powers could no longer return.'

That same week the wife of a good friend came to me for counselling. After I had fixed her a cup of tea she began to tell me about all the people who had prayed for her, yet she was still experiencing horrible dreams at night.

I interrupted her conversation and drew a circle on a piece of paper. 'Mary,' I said, 'do you have unconfessed sin in your life? Is this the reason the circle is still open?'

Mary said nothing, sitting with her head down, her hands tightly clasped in her lap, her feet together. I could see there was a strong battle going on in her life — a battle between spiritual forces.

'Do you really want to be free?' I urged.

'Oh, yes,' she said.

Suddenly she began telling me about a strong hatred she had for her mother. Everyone thought she loved her mother, but inside there were things that caused her actually to want to kill her. Yet, even as she spoke, I saw freedom coming into her eyes.

She finished her confession and then quickly asked Jesus to forgive her and cleanse her with His blood. I looked into her eyes and commanded the demon of hatred to leave in the name of Jesus.

What joy! What freedom!

Mary raised her hands in victory and began to praise the Lord, thanking Him for the liberation and forgiveness He had given her. Then she reached over and embraced me in a hug so tight I thought she would crack my ribs.

'Dear Lord,' she prayed, 'I thank You for closing the circle with Your blood.'

Having thus learned to close the circle by confessing my sins, I wish I could say that ever since then the circle has remained closed in my life. It is not so. For since Satan comes against us so often, then it is necessary to confess often, also. Regardless of how old a person may be, or how long he has ministered in the Name of Jesus Christ, that man still needs to confess his sins again and again — and ask forgiveness.

This truth became painfully clear to me recently when I was invited to Washington, D.C., to speak to a luncheon of businessmen and women. I love to talk to businessmen and was very excited about the meeting. When I arrived, however, I found only women present. This upset me for I felt that men needed to hear the message of forgiveness also.

After the meeting a fine-looking lady came up to me. 'I am in charge of arranging the programme for the world convention of our ladies' group,' she said. 'Some of the most influential women in the world will be present. Would you come to speak to us in San Francisco?'

I was still miffed that no men had been present for the luncheon. It's not that I disapprove of women's meetings. But I am concerned when men leave the spiritual activity to the women. God is calling *men*. Thus, I gave her a short, discourteous answer. 'No, I will not. I must speak to men also. I don't like this business of all women.'

She was very gracious. 'Don't you feel that you are the right person?' she asked.

'No,' I said, 'I am not the right person. I do not like this American system where men go about their business leaving the women to act like Christians. I will not come.' I turned and walked away.

Later that afternoon I was in my room, packing to catch the plane. The Lord began dealing with me. 'You were very rude to that woman,' He told me.

I argued with the Lord. 'But Lord, I feel that Your message is for all people, not just the women.'

'You were very rude to that woman,' He said again, gently.

He was right, of course. He always is. I had been speaking on forgiveness, but was unwilling to ask forgiveness for myself. I knew I was going to have to go to that gracious woman and apologize — confess my sin. Until I did, the circle would be open in my life and Satan would be pouring in many other dark thoughts as well.

I looked at my watch and saw I had only enough time to finish my packing and get to the airport. It made no difference. If I left Washington without closing the circle, I would be no good anywhere else. I would just have to miss my plane.

I called the front desk and found which room the woman was in. Then I went to her room. 'I must ask your forgiveness,' I said as she opened the door. 'I spoke to you rudely.'

She was embarrassed and tried to pass it off. 'Oh, no,' she said, 'you were not unkind. I understand perfectly. I, too, feel that men should be the spiritual leaders, not women.'

She was returning my unkindness with kindness, but that was not what I needed. I needed for her to admit that I was wrong about not speaking to women, and forgive me. I know it is often more difficult to forgive than to ask forgiveness, but it is equally important. To withhold forgiveness often leaves another person in bondage, unable to close the circle, and thus open to further attacks from Satan. It is as important to forgive as it is to ask forgiveness.

This sensitive woman understood. Reaching out and tenderly touching my hand, she said, 'I understand, Tante Corrie. I forgive you for your remarks about women's groups and I forgive you for being unkind to me.'

That was what I needed to hear. In the future I would indeed speak to women's groups. I would also keep a watch on my lips when tempted to speak unkindly. I missed my plane, but the circle was closed.

*And there came a certain poor widow, and she
threw in two mites . . . And [he] saith unto
them, Verily I say unto you, That this poor
widow hath cast more in, than all they which
have cast into the treasury: For all they did
cast in of their abundance; but she of her want
did cast in all that she had, even all her living.*

Mark 12:42–44

31   One Finger for His Glory

We arrived at her apartment by night in order to escape
detection. We were in Russia (in the region of Lithuania, on
the Baltic Sea). Ellen and I had climbed the steep stairs,
coming through a small back door into the one-room apartment. It was jammed with furniture, evidence that the old
couple had once lived in a much larger and much finer
house.

The old woman was lying on a small sofa, propped up by
pillows. Her body was bent and twisted almost beyond rec-
ognition by the dread disease of multiple sclerosis. Her aged
husband spent all his time caring for her since she was
unable to move off the sofa.

I walked across the room and kissed her wrinkled cheek.
She tried to look up but the muscles in her neck were at-
rophied so she could only roll her eyes upward and smile.
She raised her right hand, slowly, in jerks. It was the only
part of her body she could control and with her gnarled and
deformed knuckles she caressed my face. I reached over and
kissed the index finger of that hand, for it was with this one
finger that she had so long glorified God.

174

Beside her couch was a vintage typewriter. Each morning her faithful husband would rise, praising the Lord. After caring for his wife's needs and feeding her a simple breakfast, he would prop her into a sitting position on the couch, placing pillows all around her so she wouldn't topple over. Then he would move that ancient black typewriter in front of her on a small table. From an old cupboard he would remove a stack of cheap yellow paper. Then, with that blessed one finger, she would begin to type.

All day and far into the night she would type. She translated Christian books into Russian, Latvian, and the language of her people. Always using just that one finger — peck ... peck ... peck — she typed out the pages. Portions of the Bible, the books of Billy Graham, Watchman Nee and Corrie ten Boom — all came from her typewriter. That was why I was there — to thank her.

She was hungry to hear news about these men of God she had never met, yet whose books she had so faithfully translated. We talked about Watchman Nee, who was then in a prison in China, and I told her all I knew of his life and ministry. I also told her of the wonderful ministry of Billy Graham and of the many people who were giving their lives to the Lord.

'Not only does she translate their books,' her husband said as he hovered close by during our conversation, 'but she prays for these men every day while she types. Sometimes it takes a long time for her finger to hit the key, or for her to get the paper in the machine, but all the time she is praying for those whose books she is working on.'

I looked at her wasted form on the sofa, her head pulled down and her feet curled back under her body. 'Oh, Lord, why don't You heal her?' I cried inwardly.

Her husband, sensing my anguish of soul, gave the answer. 'God has a purpose in her sickness. Every other

Christian in the city is watched by the secret police. But because she has been sick so long, no one ever looks in on her. They leave us alone and she is the only person in all the city who can type quietly, undetected by the police.'

I looked around at the tiny room, so jammed full of furniture from better days. In one corner was the kitchen. Beside the cupboard was her husband's 'office', a battered desk where he sorted the pages that came from her typewriter to pass them on to the Christians. I thought of Jesus sitting over against the treasury, and my heart leaped for joy as I heard Jesus bless this sick old woman who, like the widow, had given all she had.

What a warrior!

> When she enters the beautiful city
> And the saved all around her appear,
> Many people around will tell her:
> It was you that invited me here.

AUTHOR UNKNOWN

Ellen and I returned to Holland where we were able to obtain a new typewriter and have it shipped to her. Now she could make carbon copies of her translations.

Today we got a letter from her husband. In the early morning hours last week she left to be with the Lord. But, he said, she had worked up until midnight that same night, typing with that one finger to the glory of God.

*Haven't you yet learned that your body is the
home of the Holy Spirit God gave you, and
that he lives within you? Your own body does
not belong to you. For God has bought you
with a great price. So use every part of your
body to give glory back to God, because he
owns it.*

1 Corinthians 6:19, 20 LB

32 The Ding-Dong Principle

In Holland we have many churches with belfries. The bells
in the steeples are rung by hand, with a rope that is pulled
from the vestibule of the church.

One day a young Flemish girl, who had repented and
received deliverance from lust and impurity, came to me
while I was speaking in one of these churches.

'Even though I have been delivered,' she said, 'at night I
still keep dreaming of my old way of life. I am afraid I will
slip back into Satan's grasp.'

'Up in that church tower,' I said, nodding towards the
belfry, 'is a bell which is rung by pulling on a rope. But you
know what? After the sexton lets go of the rope, the bell
keeps on swinging. First *ding*, then *dong*. Slower and slower
until there's a final *dong* and it stops.

'I believe the same thing is true of deliverance. When the
demons are cast out in the name of the Lord Jesus Christ, or
when sin is confessed and renounced, then Satan's hand is
removed from the rope. But if we worry about our past
bondage, Satan will use this opportunity to keep the echoes
ringing in our minds.'

A sweet light spread across the girl's face. 'You mean even though I sometimes have temptations, that I am still free, that Satan is no longer pulling the rope which controls my life?'

'The purity of your life is evidence of your deliverance,' I said. 'You should not worry about the *dings* and the *dongs*, they are nothing but echoes.'

Demons seldom leave without leaving behind their vibrations — *dings* and *dongs*. It is as though they give the clapper one big swing on the way out, scaring us into thinking they are still there. They know that, even though they have to flee at the Name of Jesus, if we grow fearful over the remaining echoes, other demons can come in and take their place.

The same is true of forgiveness. When we forgive someone, we take our hand off the rope. But if we've been tugging at our grievances for a long time, we mustn't be surprised when the old angry thoughts keep coming up for a while. They're just the *ding-dongs* of the old bell slowing down.

The Bible promises that after we confess and denounce our sins, God cleanses us from them by the blood of Jesus. Indeed, He says, 'Your sins and iniquities will I remember no more' (*See* Hebrews 8:12). However, we can do something God cannot do. We can remember our old sins. These are the *dings* and the *dongs* of our past life. When we hear them we need to remember that through Jesus' sacrifice on Calvary, Satan can no longer pull the rope in our life. We may be tempted. We may even fall back occasionally. But we have been delivered from the bondage of sin, and even though the vibrations may still sound in our lives, they will grow less and less and eventually stop completely.

Once Satan has been cast out of the house of your life, he cannot return as long as you walk in obedience. Your body is the temple of the Holy Spirit. However, that does not prevent him (or his demons) from standing outside the house and shouting through the windows, saying, 'We're still here!'

But, hallelujah, we know Satan for who he is — the prince of liars. He is *not* still here — he has been cast out. So whenever you hear one of those old echoes in your life — one of the *dings* or *dongs* — you need to stop right then and say, 'Thank You, Jesus. You have bought me with Your blood and sin has no right to sound off in my life.'

And when you stand praying, if you have a grievance against anyone, forgive him, so that your Father in heaven may forgive you the wrongs you have done.

Mark 11:25 NEB

33 The Blacks and Whites of Forgiveness

I wish I could say that after a long and fruitful life, travelling the world, I had learned to forgive all my enemies. I wish I could say that merciful and charitable thoughts just naturally flowed from me and on to others. But they don't. If there is one thing I've learned since I've passed my eightieth birthday, it's that I can't store up good feelings and behaviour — but only draw them fresh from God each day.

Maybe I'm glad it's that way, for every time I go to Him, He teaches me something else. I recall the time — and I was almost seventy — when some Christian friends whom I loved and trusted did something which hurt me. You would have thought that, having been able to forgive the guards in Ravensbruck, forgiving Christian friends would be child's play. It wasn't. For weeks I seethed inside. But at last I asked God again to work His miracle in me. And again it happened: first the cold-blooded decision, then the flood of joy and peace. I had forgiven my friends; I was restored to my Father.

Then, why was I suddenly awake in the middle of the night, rehashing the whole affair again? *My friends!* I thought. *People I loved.* If it had been strangers. I wouldn't have minded so.

I sat up and switched on the light. 'Father, I thought it was all forgiven. Please help me do it.'

But the next night I woke up again. They'd talked so sweetly too! Never a hint of what they were planning. 'Father!' I cried in alarm. 'Help me!'

Then it was that another secret of forgiveness became evident. It is not enough to simply say, 'I forgive you.' I must also begin to live it out. And in my case, that meant acting as though their sins, like mine, were buried in the depths of the deepest sea. If God could remember them no more — and He had said, '[Your] sins and iniquities will I remember no more' (Hebrews 10:17) — then neither should I. And the reason the thoughts kept coming back to me was that I kept turning their sin over in my mind.

And so I discovered another of God's principles: We can trust God not only for our emotions but also for our thoughts. As I asked Him to renew my mind, He also took away my thoughts. He still had more to teach me, however, even from this single episode. Many years later, after I had passed my eightieth birthday, an American friend came to visit me in Holland. As we sat in my little apartment in Baarn he asked me about those people from long ago who had taken advantage of me.

'It is nothing,' I said a little smugly. 'It is all forgiven.'

'By you, yes,' he said. 'But what about them? Have they accepted your forgiveness?'

'They say there is nothing to forgive! They deny it ever happened. No matter what they say, though, I can prove they were wrong.' I went eagerly to my desk. 'See, I have it in black and white! I saved all their letters and I can show you where . . .'

'Corrie!' My friend slipped his arm through mine and gently closed the drawer. 'Aren't you the one whose sins are at the bottom of the sea? Yet are the sins of your friends etched in black and white?'

For an astonishing moment I could not find my voice. 'Lord Jesus,' I whispered at last, 'who takes all my sins away, forgive me for preserving all these years the evidence against others! Give me grace to burn all the blacks and whites as a sweet-smelling sacrifice to Your glory.'

I did not go to sleep that night until I had gone through my desk and pulled out those letters — curling now with age — and fed them all into my little coal-burning grate. As the flames leaped and glowed, so did my heart. 'Forgive us our trespasses,' Jesus taught us to pray, 'as we forgive those who trespass against us.' In the ashes of those letters I was seeing yet another facet of His mercy. What more He would teach me about forgiveness in the days ahead I didn't know, but tonight's was good news enough.

Forgiveness is the key which unlocks the door of resentment and the handcuffs of hatred. It breaks the chains of bitterness and the shackles of selfishness. The forgiveness of Jesus not only takes away our sins, it makes them as if they had never been.

. . . Even so, come, Lord Jesus.

Revelation 22:20

34 Getting Ready for the End

Some time ago, I was with a group of students in the midwest. Some of them were new Christians, but most of them did not know the Lord. They were interested in all kinds of other things, and a Christian professor had organized weekly meetings to answer their questions. So it was that at the last evening meeting of that semester the professor said, 'Now you can hear something about Christianity in practice.'

First I spoke to those who were Christians. 'How long have you known Jesus?' I asked.

One said, 'Two weeks.' Another said, 'Three years.' And still another answered and said, 'I met Him only yesterday.'

Then I said to them, 'Well, I have good news. I have known Him seventy-five years, and I can tell you something, men. He will never let you down.'

Next I told the other students about Jesus Christ, and what He had done for me, and the great miracles also. When He tells you to love your enemies, He gives you the love that He demands from you. They were listening intently, and I was led by the Holy Spirit not to go into any doctrines or teachings other than the reality of Jesus Christ. I told them of the joy of having Jesus with me, whatever happened, and how I knew from experience that the light of Jesus is stronger than the greatest darkness. I told them of the darkness of my prison experiences, realizing that only those people who were in a German concentration camp could ever fully understand. However, I wanted these students to know that, even though I was there where every day six hundred people either died or were killed, when Jesus is with you the worst can happen and the best remains.

Afterwards the students came up and we had coffee. One said to me, 'I would love to ask Jesus to come into my heart, but I cannot. I am a Jew.'

I said, 'You cannot ask Jesus into your heart because you are a Jew? Then you do not understand that with the Jew (Jesus) in your heart — you are a double Jew.'

He said, 'Oh, then it is possible?'

'On the divine side He was God's Son. On the human side He was a Jew. When you accept Him you do not become a Gentile. You become even more Jewish than before. You will be a completed Jew.'

With great joy the boy received the Lord Jesus as his Saviour.

There is a great new surge of interest in spiritual things. Many are interested in Jesus Christ who have never shown any interest before. Churches — which have been dead and cold like mausoleums — are coming to life. All across the world many are being saved and being filled with the Holy Spirit.

At the same time, however, many others are turning away from God. They are openly worshiping Satan. Many others are calling themselves Christians, but are involved in the occult, fortune telling, astrology, mind science, and other things of Satan.

I see over the whole world that there are two huge armies marching — the army of the Antichrist and the army of Jesus Christ. We know from the Bible that Jesus Christ will have the victory, but now the Antichrist is preparing for the time that will come before Jesus returns. The Bible says there will be a time of tribulation, and the Antichrist will take over the whole world. He will be a very 'good, religious' man, and he will make one religion for the whole world. After it has been arranged, he will proclaim himself as its god. The Bible prophesies that the time will come when we cannot buy or sell, unless we bear the sign of the Antichrist; that means that world money is coming, and people know this today. If I did not believe in the Bible before, I should believe in it now. Because what was foretold in the Bible you can now read in the newspapers.

At a student meeting in California a theological student approached me saying, 'What's all this talk about Jesus' coming again? Don't you know that men have been prophesying for years that He would come, and He never has. Even the early church could not live their religion because they were too busy looking for Christ to return. He is not coming back. It is all foolishness.'

I looked at the young man. He was so smug, so full of scoffing, and I felt sorry for him.

'Indeed, Jesus is coming again, and soon,' I said. 'And you have just proved it to me.'

He blinked his eyes. 'How did I prove it to you?'

'Because the Bible talks about it in 2 Peter 3:3, that in the last days there shall come scoffers walking after their own lusts and they will say, "Where is the promise of His Coming? Ever since the early church men have been looking for Him and He has not come." So you see, my young friend, you are one of the signs of His Coming.'

I am not afraid when I think about the Coming of the

185

Lord Jesus. Instead I welcome it. I do not know whether it would be better for me to die and be among that great host of saints who will return with Him, or whether it would be better to remain here and listen for the sound of the trumpet. Either way I like the words of the song that says:

> God is working His purpose out,
> As year succeeds to year:
> God is working His purpose out
> And the time is drawing near —
> Nearer and nearer draws the time
> The time that shall surely be,
> When the earth shall be filled with
>   the glory of God
> As the waters cover the sea.

A. C. AINGER

I find that when Communists speak of the future of the world, they show a pattern for peace through communism. But when I ask them, 'What about when you die?' they say, 'Then everything is ended. There is no life after this life.' The Bible tells us that the Antichrist can imitate much, even the gifts of the Spirit. But there is one thing he cannot imitate, and that is the peace of God which passes all understanding.

But there are *good* things to tell about the future of the world. For instance, the Bible says the Tree of Life will be used for the healing of the nations. This means that there will be *nations* to heal, and there will be *healing*. I am so thankful that we have the Bible and can know the future of God's plan.

As the end times draw closer and closer, so does the power of God grow greater and greater. One day, on a trip to Russia, I approached the customs officer with a suitcase full of Russian Bibles. I stood in the line and saw how carefully the customs officers checked every suitcase. Suddenly a great fear swept over me. 'What will he do when he finds my Bibles? Send me back to Holland? Put me in prison?'

I closed my eyes to shut out the scene around me and said, 'Lord, in Jeremiah 1, it is written that "God watches over his word to perform it" (*See* v. 12). Lord, the Bibles in my suitcase are Your Word. Now, God, please watch over Your Word — my Bibles — so I may take them to Your people in Russia.'

Now I know that is not what Jeremiah meant, but I have found that if I pray with my hand on the promises of the open Bible that I do not have to wait until my position is doctrinally sound. God sees my heart.

The moment I prayed I opened my eyes and saw around my suitcase light beings. They were angels. It was the first and only time in my life that I had ever seen them, although I had known many, many times they were present. But this time I saw them, only for a moment, and then they were gone. But so was my fear.

I moved on through the customs line, sliding my suitcase along the stainless steel table toward the officer who was doing such a thorough inspection. At last I was before him.

'Is this your suitcase?' he asked.

'Yes, sir,' I answered politely.

'It seems very heavy,' he said, grasping it by the handle and picking it up.

'It is very heavy,' I said.

He smiled. 'Since you are the last one to come through the line I now have time to help you. If you will follow me I shall carry it for you out to your taxi.'

My heart almost overflowed with hallelujahs as I followed

him through the customs gate and right out to the street where he helped me get a taxi to the hotel.

So, even though we are rapidly approaching the time when the Antichrist will try to take over the world, I am not afraid. For I have an even greater promise of the constant Presence of Jesus who is greater than anything Satan can throw against me.

The Apostle Peter said, 'Because, my dear friends, you have a hope like this before you, I urge you to make certain that such a day will find you at peace with God and man, clean and blameless in his sight' (2 Peter 3:14 PHILLIPS).

Surrender to the Lord Jesus Christ must not be partial — but total. Only when we repent and turn away from our sins (using His power, of course) does He fill us with His Holy Spirit. The fruit of the Holy Spirit makes us right with God and God's love in us makes us right with men. Through that we can forgive — even love — our enemies.

Jesus Himself makes us ready for His Coming.

Adapted from Agape Power #2, Copyright 1972. Logos Journal, 185 North Avenue, Plainfield, N.J. 07060. Reprinted with permission.

> *. . . Suffer little children, and forbid them not,*
> *to come unto me: for of such is the kingdom*
> *of heaven.*
>
> Matthew 19:14

35   Little Witness for Christ

Tante Jans lost her husband before she was forty years old. He had been a well-known minister in Rotterdam and she had worked faithfully beside him in the church. They had no children and after he died it was clear that her place was to be in our house in Haarlem. She was a poet, author, and organizer — especially was she an organizer! Soon after she moved into the Beje she started a club for girls where she led the meetings and began publishing a small monthly paper for them.

It was long before World War I started, but a detachment of Dutch soldiers was stationed in Haarlem. Seeing many soldiers in the streets, Tante Jans decided to open a club for them too. She approached some wealthy people and within a short time had enough money to build a military home. Twice a week Tante Jans went to the house to lead in a Bible study.

Tante Jans also invited the soldiers to come to our house. Since they were lonely and did not like the street life, many of them accepted. Almost every evening we had soldiers in our home.

One sergeant was a great musician and Tante Jans asked

him to teach me and my sister Nollie to play the harmonium — an old pump organ. It wasn't long before I was joining Tante Jans at the military home to accompany the singing.

One night, in my eleventh year, a large group of soldiers had gathered for the Bible study. Before I played, Tante Jans made me sing. The song I sang was about the lost sheep which was found by the shepherd. I sang it slowly and dramatically, climaxing it with the last line:

And the sheep that went astray was me.

As I finished singing a big blond Dutch officer reached out and pulled me to him. Picking me up and sitting me on his knee, he laughed and said, 'Tell me, young lady, how did you go astray?'

All the other soldiers laughed, and I was red with embarrassment. It did seem odd that such a little girl would describe herself as a lost sheep.

I had to confess that the line just belonged to the song and that I had never, never been a lost sheep. Then I told him that as a little girl, just five years of age, I had given my heart to Jesus Christ and could never remember not having belonged to Him.

The officer grew very serious and his eyes filled with tears. 'Ah, that is the way it should be, little Sweet-Face,' he said solemnly. 'How much better to come to Jesus as a little child, than to have to stumble, as I have, always seeking the shepherd.'

Then he closed his eyes and said softly, 'But tonight I think I shall stop seeking, and let Him find me instead.'

That night there was deep joy in the Bible meeting. The Lord had used me to lead a man to Christ. It was the first time in my life, and it had taken place not because of what I

said, but because of the Holy Spirit who was in me. It was a
secret I have remembered all the years of my life as I have
travelled the world — a tramp for the Lord.